EDUCATION
AND PEACE

EDUCATION AND PEACE

MARIA MONTESSORI

Translated by Helen R. Lane

HENRY REGNERY COMPANY • CHICAGO

This translation has been prepared in cooperation with A. M. Joosten,
Director, Indian Montessori Training Courses (AMI).

CONTENTS

Foreword   vii

Preface   xi

Part I: Foundations for Peace

1 Peace   3

2 For Peace   27

3 Educate for Peace   32

**Part II: Educate for Peace, Sixth International
Montessori Congress**

4 Address Opening the Congress   41

5 Why May Education Have an Influence on the World
   Today?   46

6 Second Lecture   55

7 The Form Education Must Take to Be Able to Help the
   World in Our Present Circumstances   63

8 The Need for Universal Accord So That Man May Be
   Morally Trained to Defend Humanity   70

9 Fifth Lecture   77

10 Lecture Closing the Congress   84

11 My Method   90

Part III: The Importance of Education in Bringing About Peace

12 First Lecture   101

13 Supernature and the Single Nation   109

14 The Education of the Individual   119

Part IV: Address to the World Fellowship of Faiths

15 Educate for Peace   137

Foreword

Maria Montessori's tireless efforts to open new paths were as irresistible as a force of nature.

When, as a doctor, she found herself involved by chance in the treatment of physically and mentally abnormal children, she worked with them in a spirit of absolute self-dedication. Seven years later, providence brought her into contact with a group of normal children of preschool age. For them she inaugurated the first *Casa dei Bambini* (House of the Children) in Rome on January 6, 1907. The psychological manifestations of these children, who revealed personality characteristics that had not hitherto been taken into consideration and that had evidently been prevented from revealing themselves by the oppression of traditional education in home and school, taught her unsuspected truths. These truths she verified through repeated experiment and through her work with children of diverse social and cultural backgrounds all over the world. She shed brilliant light on her discoveries through intuitive insights that bore the mark of genius. Once a firm basis for her theories had been established through practical experience, her thoughts as an educator and a philosopher ranged further and unveiled new perspectives that seem broader and broader as time goes by.

The aim of all of Maria Montessori's writings was to bring

about a new understanding of the potentialities and needs of children, particularly in their earliest years, and to present a thoroughgoing critique of the errors and prejudices of the past, though in no sense a sterile or negative one.

In 1932 it became difficult for her to pursue her work in Italy; in 1934 the doors of her homeland closed behind her. From that date on, her reputation, which seemed to grow dimmer in Italy, glowed more and more brightly abroad.

Once outside Italy, the threat of war—feared by everyone in Europe—began to weigh heavily upon her. Her profound concern did not stem from the political problem of war, but rather from the human problem. It moved her deeply, the same way the problem of the early years of childhood had haunted her in her youth. Her impressive mental powers once again had been called forth. Just as her experience with children had inspired her to uncover the laws of human development, so the problem of war now caused her to engage in a passionate search for new human truths. Taking as a point of departure her firm conviction that the child must be our teacher and her ideas regarding the free, harmonious, and balanced development of the individual human being, she moved on to consider the problems of human and social development and began a crusade in the name of education: "Establishing a lasting peace is the work of education; all politics can do is keep us out of war."

As illuminating as flashes of lightning, her ideas brought hope to the countries of Europe. Political groups and associations rallied around her, embracing her faith in education and in the redemption to which children could lead the way. When Maria Montessori brought up the words *peace* and *war*, the concepts became targets of a new spirit of criticism that broke down the obsolete, traditional ways of thinking about them and that brought to light a new kind of truth better

suited to modern thought. Maria Montessori examined this
new problem with the same honest and penetrating attention
that had always marked her search for truth.

In 1932, in a far-reaching speech that appears in this vol-
ume, she discussed the problem of peace at the International
Office of Education in Geneva, which was at that time the
European center of the peace movement.

In 1936 a European peace congress was organized to deal
with political aspects of the problem. At the congress, held in
Brussels, Maria Montessori again delivered lectures on peace,
as did other eminent European political spokesmen. After
fleeing to London at the outbreak of the civil war in Spain,
she gave speeches on peace in England.

In 1937 the Danish government offered the Montessori
movement the use of the hall of the Parliament in
Copenhagen for a major congress entitled "Educate for
Peace." Dr. Montessori dealt with the subject of the moral
defense of humanity in a series of lectures to the
congress.

Under the auspices of the Utrecht Scientific Society, she delivered three lectures before the International School of Philosophy in December, 1937. And in July, 1939, as the
warclouds grew darker, she delivered a lecture before the
World Fellowship of Faiths, an international religious organization.

Maria Montessori shed genuine light on social, political,
scientific, and religious thought. Universities, organizations,
and associations in many different countries, united in their
determination to restructure human society, proposed her as
a candidate for the Nobel Peace Prize in 1949 and 1950.

Maria Montessori's many years of unhindered, dedicated
work in India, beginning in 1939, gave a scientific basis to
her thoughts about the restructuring of society and about

peace and enabled her to build the solid and cohesive philosophy put before her readers in her definitive work, *The Absorbent Mind.*

We have collected here those lectures in which she first comes to grips with the great problem of the future of humanity, in which she first gives passionate expression to her insights on the subject.

All those who are curious to know why Maria Montessori was proposed as a candidate for the Nobel Peace Prize and received votes from all over the world will discover in this collection of public addresses many links in the chain of her thought as it developed and her activity as it unfolded and see here the first traces of the deep imprint left by her powerful mind.

THE EDITORS OF THE ITALIAN EDITION

Preface

The question of peace cannot be discussed properly from a merely negative point of view, as politics ordinarily regards it, in the narrow sense of avoiding war and resolving conflicts between nations without recourse to violence.

Inherent in the very meaning of the word *peace* is the positive notion of constructive social reform. It is a commonplace that we must create a different sort of man in order to have a different sort of society, but this remains no more than an abstraction. Although it is quite true that man as an individual can improve and that society can be based on principles of justice and love, all of us are aware that these goals do not constitute a reality just beyond our grasp but rather an aspiration whose fulfillment lies far in the future.

There is one concrete and immediate fact, nonetheless, that should be considered from the point of view of peace—the fact that human society has not yet achieved the form of organization necessary to confront its present needs. There is compelling reason, therefore, to turn our attention to the necessities of the present rather than to the organization of a better future.

Society at present does not adequately prepare man for civic life; there is no "moral organization" of the masses. Human beings are brought up to regard themselves as isolated individuals who must satisfy their immediate needs by competing with other individuals. A powerful campaign of organization would be required to enable men to understand and structure social phenomena, to propose and pursue collective ends, and thus to bring about orderly social progress.

But today all we have is an organization of *things* and no organization of mankind. Only the *environment* is organized. Technical progress has set in motion a sort of awesome "mechanism" that catches individuals up in its toils, attracting them as a magnet attracts iron filings. This is true, moreover, of both manual workers and intellectuals. Each person is set apart from every other by his own private interests; everyone wants only some sort of work that will satisfy his material needs; everyone is attracted by and trapped in the interlocking gears of a mechanized and bureaucratic world. It is obvious that mechanisms alone cannot make man progress, for progress depends on man. And eventually a time must come when humanity assumes control of progress and gives it direction.

That time has come. Either mankind as a whole will organize and master the mechanical world, or the mechanical world will destroy humanity.

To achieve the formidably difficult goal—the universal cooperation required of humanity for continued progress—mankind must organize. It is urgently necessary for all men to participate and to remedy a defect that endangers the very existence of civilization. *Humanity must be organized,* for the frontier that is weakest, the frontier that will yield first and allow the enemy—that is, war—to enter, is not a physical boundary between one nation and another, but man's lack of preparation and the isolation of the individual. We must develop the spiritual life of man and then organize humanity for peace. The positive aspect of peace lies in the restructuring of human society on a scientific basis. Social peace and harmony can have only one foundation: man himself.

Reconstruction—that is, a stable and well-structured social order—is not even considered when society is viewed practically, for such a view is inherently conservative. It is obvious, however, that the sudden and amazing changes that have taken place in the organization of man's material environment in the last fifty years as a result of scientific discoveries have brought about such radically altered conditions in men's lives that it is now absolutely imperative to give serious thought to the human side of things in order to help men themselves change for the better.

This is the task of education.

Education today is still confined by the limits of a social order that is now past. Education today not only is contrary to the dictates of science; it also runs counter to the social needs of our time. Education cannot be dismissed as an insignificant factor in people's lives, as a means of furnishing a few rudiments of culture to young people. It must be viewed first of all from the perspective of the development of human values in the individual, in particular his moral values, and second from the point of view of organizing the individuals possessed of these enhanced values into a society consciously aware of its destiny. A new form of morality must accompany this new form of civilization. Order and discipline must be aimed at the attainment of human harmony, and any act that hinders the establishment of a genuine community of all mankind must be regarded as immoral and a threat to the life of society.

This end cannot be achieved without practical and concrete effort. It is not enough to preach an abstract principle or to attempt to persuade others. A "great work" must be undertaken. An extremely important social task lies before us: actuating man's value, allowing him to attain the maximum development of his energies, truly preparing him to bring about a different form of human society on a higher plane. Social man cannot be created all at once out of nothing. The individual has grown to adulthood after being repressed, isolated, and led to pursue only his own personal interests throughout childhood and adolescence, under the blind domination of adults who are only too inclined to neglect the values of life and set him only the petty and selfish goal of getting a good job for himself within the social order.

Education today causes the individual to dry up and his spiritual values to wither away. He becomes a cipher, a cog in the blind machine that his environment represents. Such preparation for life has been absurd in every age; today it is a crime, a sin. And education that represses and rejects the promptings of the moral self, that erects obstacles and barriers in the way of the development of intelligence, that condemns huge sectors of the population to ignorance is a crime. Since all our riches come from man's labor, it is absurd not to regard man himself as the most fundamental of our riches. We must seek out, we must cultivate, we must enhance the value of man's energies, his intelligence, his creative spirit, his moral powers so that nothing is lost. Man's moral energies in particular must be turned to account. For he is not only a producer. He is also called upon to assume and fulfill a mission in the universe. What man produces must be directed toward an end that we might call *civilization*, or, in other words, the creation of a supernature as the handiwork of humanity! But man must become aware of his own greatness; he must consciously make himself the master of the world outside him and of human events.

The special province of morality is the relation between

individuals, and it is the very basis of social life. Morality must be regarded as the science of organizing a society of men whose highest value is their selfhood and not the efficiency of their machines. Men must learn how to participate consciously in the social discipline that orders all their functions within society and how to help keep these functions in balance.

The crux of the question of peace and war thus no longer lies in the need to give men the material weapons to defend the geographical frontiers separating nation from nation, for the real first line of defense against war is man himself, and where man is socially disorganized and devalued, the universal enemy will enter the breach.

I
Foundations for Peace

1   Peace

Introduction

It seems odd and somehow not in keeping with the spirit of this age of specialization that I should be called upon to discuss peace, a subject that, were it to become a special discipline, would be the most noble one of all, for the very life of humanity depends on it. So also, perhaps, does the question of whether our entire civilization evolves or disappears.

It is quite strange, in fact, that as yet there is no such thing as a science of peace, since the science of war appears to be highly advanced, at least regarding such concrete subjects as armaments and strategy. As a collective human phenomenon, however, even war involves a mystery, for all the peoples of the earth, who profess to be eager to banish war as the worst of scourges, are nonetheless the very ones who concur in the starting of wars and who willingly support armed combat. Confronted with the question of natural disasters against which man is powerless, many scholars passionately devote themselves to the study of the hidden causes responsible for such phenomena. War is a human phenomenon and should thus be all the more accessible to inquiring human minds.

This address was given at the International Office of Education in Geneva in 1932.

Since this has not proved to be the case, we must conclude that humanity's achievement of world peace is linked to complex indirect factors, which are unquestionably worthy of study and capable of becoming the objects of a powerful science.

One is struck by the fact that man has been able to unravel so many mysteries of the universe, to detect hidden energies and harness them for his own use, impelled by his instinct to preserve life and, even more important, by his deeply rooted drive to learn and to acquire knowledge. At the same time, however, man's investigations of his own inner energies have left a vast abyss, and his mastery of them has been almost nil. This master of the external world has not managed to tame his own inner energies, which have accumulated through the centuries and have been loosely organized in various great human groups. If man were asked the reasons for this paradox, he would be unable to provide any clear answer. As for peace, it has never been the object of an orderly and ongoing process of investigation that goes by the name of a science; on the contrary, a clear concept of peace does not figure among the countless ideas that enrich our human awareness.

War and Peace

What is generally meant by the word *peace* is the cessation of war. But this negative concept is not an adequate description of genuine peace. Most important, if we observe the apparent aim of a war, peace understood in this sense represents, rather, the ultimate and permanent triumph of war. The primary motive of the wars of antiquity, in fact, was the conquest of land and the consequent subjugation of entire peoples.

Although man's environment is no longer the actual physical land but rather the social organization in and of itself, resting on economic structures, territorial conquest is still regarded as the real reason for which wars are waged, and throngs of men still are swept off their feet and troop to the colors under the influence of the suggestion of conquest.

Now, why do great numbers of men march off to face death when their homeland is threatened with the specter of invasion? And why do not only men, but also women and even children, hasten to defend their country? Out of fear of what will go by the name of peace once the war is over.

Human history teaches us that *peace* means the forcible submission of the conquered to domination once the invader has consolidated his victory, the loss of everything the vanquished hold dear, and the end of their enjoyment of the fruits of their labor and their conquests. The vanquished are forced to make sacrifices, as if they are the only ones who are guilty and merit punishment, simply because they have been defeated. Meanwhile, the victors flaunt the rights they feel they have won over the defeated populace, who remain the victims of the disaster. Such conditions may mark the end of actual combat, but they certainly cannot be called peace. The real moral scourge stems in fact from this very set of circumstances.

If I may be allowed to make a comparison, war might be likened to the burning of a palace filled with works of art and precious treasures. When the palace is reduced to a heap of smoldering ashes and suffocating smoke, the physical disaster is complete; but the smoldering ashes, the smoke that prevents people from breathing, can be compared to peace as the world ordinarily understands it.

This is the same sort of peace that ensues after a man catches a disease, after a war is waged in his body between his vital energies and the invading microorganisms, and after the man eventually loses the battle and dies. We very appropriately express the hope that the dead man will rest in peace. But what a difference between this sort of peace and the peace that goes by the name of good health!

The fact that we mistakenly call the permanent triumph of the aims of a war "peace" causes us to fail to recognize the way to salvation, the path that could lead us to true peace. And since the history of every people on earth is marked by one wave after another of such triumphs and such forms of injustice, as long as such a profound misunderstanding continues to exist, peace will definitely fail to fall within the range of human possibilities. I am not speaking only of the past, for even today the lives of peoples who are not at war represent an acceptance of the situation created between victor and vanquished. The former wreak merciless havoc, and the latter curse their fate like the devils and the damned in Dante's *Inferno*. Both are far from the divine influence of love; all of them are fallen creatures, for whom universal harmony has been shattered into a thousand pieces. And this chain of events continues to repeat itself, for all peoples have been alternately victors and vanquished and have wasted their energies in this terrible ebb and flow of their fortunes in the boundless tides of the centuries.

We must bring the profound difference, the contrary moral aims of war and peace, into the clear light of day. Otherwise we shall wander about blindly, the victims of our delusions, and in our search for peace we shall come across nothing but bloody weapons and destitution. The prospect of true peace makes us turn our thoughts to the triumph of justice and love among men, to the building of a better world where harmony reigns. An orientation of our minds that clearly distinguishes between war and peace is only the starting point, however. In order to shed light on this subject, as on any other, a positive process of investigation is required. But where in the world is there a laboratory in which the human mind has endeavored to discover some part of the truth, to bring to light some positive factor with regard to the problem of peace?

Meetings inspired by the loftiest sentiments and the noblest wishes for peace have been held, it is true. But we shall never discover valid concepts on which to base a study allowing us to understand and unravel the causes of this awesome enigma unless we realize that we are faced with real moral chaos. There is no term but moral chaos to describe our spiritual situation, wherein a man who discovers a virulent microbe and the preventive serum that can save many human lives receives great praise, but wherein a man who discovers destructive techniques and directs all his intellectual powers toward the annihilation of entire peoples is praised even more highly. The concepts of the value of life and the moral principles involved in these two cases are so diametrically opposed that we must seriously consider the possibility that the collective personality of mankind is suffering from some mysterious form of schizophrenia.

Obviously there are chapters in human psychology that have yet to be written and forces that we have not yet mastered that presage enormous dangers for humanity.

Such unknown factors must become the object of scientific study. The very idea of research implies the existence of hidden or perhaps even unsuspected factors that are far removed from their ultimate effects. The causes of war cannot lie in well-known and thoroughly studied phenomena dealing with the social injustices suffered by workers in economic production, or the consequences of a war fought to the finish, because these social facts are too apparent and too easily recognizable in the light of even the most elementary logic for us to regard them as the deep-rooted or mysterious causes of war. They are rather the tip of the fuse, the last part to be ignited before the explosion that war represents.

As an illustration, consider the history of a phenomenon analogous to war, a physical phenomenon in the field of medicine that presents striking parallels. I am referring to the plague: a scourge capable of decimating and even wiping out entire peoples, a disease that was frightful because it raged unchecked in the dark shadows of the ignorance surrounding it. The plague was conquered only when its hidden causes became the object of scientific investigation.

Like wars, epidemics of the plague broke out only sporadically and were quite unpredictable. The plague, moreover, died out by itself, without active intervention on the part of men, who had no idea what caused it and who feared it as a tremendous punishment visited upon man by God, wreaking destruction no less celebrated in history than that brought about by wars. But the plague caused many more deaths and economic disasters than wars and, like wars, were often named after some illustrious historical figure. The annals of mankind therefore record a plague of Pericles, of Marcus Aurelius, of Constantine, of Gregory the Great. In the fourteenth century a plague in China caused the death of ten million people. The same terrible epidemic swept through Russia, Asia Minor, Egypt, and Europe, threatening to destroy all of humanity.

Welles quotes Hecker as estimating the total number dead at over twenty-five million—a frightful toll that no war, even the war of 1914–1918, has ever equaled. These terrible periods, in which productive labor was reduced almost to nothing, paved the way for several successive periods of horrible suffering. The scourge of starvation followed that of the plague, accompanied by a wave of insanity, for a large percentage of those who survived were mentally deranged, a calamity that made the return to normalcy even more difficult and long halted the constructive work necessary for social progress.

It is interesting to learn men's various interpretations of this colossal scourge and the means men used to defend themselves against what we may regard as a war visited on man by nature. In Homer and Livy and on down through the Latin chronicles of the Middle Ages, the interpretation is always the same: epidemics of the plague are caused by evil men who spread poisons. Describing the plague of the year 189 A.D., Dion Cassius relates that malefactors were recruited and paid money to shoot poisoned needles at people all over the Empire. In the time of Pope Clement VI large numbers of Jews accused of spreading the plague were massacred. During the siege of Naples the plague wiped out four hundred thousand inhabitants of the city—almost the entire population—and approximately three-quarters of the troops besieging the city. The Neapolitans were convinced that the French had poisoned them, and vice versa. Even more interesting are documents preserved in the *Biblioteca Ambrosiana* in Milan describing the establishment of special courts for the criminal trials of two presumed poisoners, followed by their execution as an example to the populace. This is one of the few cases in which a legal trial was conducted in order to prevent the populace, roused to fury at the death toll, from dealing its own vengeful brand of justice. The records of the proceedings, preserved in the state archives according to the rules, have been examined by many writers and interpreted in a number of ways.

It is hard for us today to imagine how something that was so obviously a contagious disease could have been regarded as evidence of murder and the supposed perpetrators tried in a court of law. Accusing two men of responsibility for the vast

numbers of deaths this epidemic caused would strike us as absurd. But, even though this seems absurd today, doesn't something similar happen with regard to war? In this case, too,
people are eager to blame the universal scourge on some individual or other—on the Kaiser, on the czarina, on the monk
Rasputin, on the man who assassinated the Archduke at
Sarajevo, or on anyone else they please.

Did not people in the days of the plague congregate in vast
throngs in public squares and churches in the hope of saving
themselves, not knowing that all this really did was spread
the disease? And when the epidemic was over, didn't the sur-
vivors joyfully begin their lives anew and smilingly reassure
themselves that the evil they had suffered was a necessary test
of man and perhaps even the very last one he would ever be
subjected to? Don't the remedies we resort to today in the
hope of escaping war recall the hopes and the false remedies
of those bygone days?

The alliances of the last war were meant to achieve a balance of power in Europe that would prevent war. But did the
alliances not on the contrary pave the way for a huge disaster,
since many countries were dragged into the conflict simply
because of pledges they had made to other nations? Even if
all the nations of the earth were to form a common alliance
today in order to avoid armed conflict, they would still
remain as blind as ever to the primary causes of war. Further-
more, there might well be armed conflict on a global scale,
since men would once again hope to bring about genuine
peace, to reach a final solution, by waging this one last war.

Without scientific methods of research, who could ever
have found the direct causes of the plague, the specific micro-
organism responsible for it, and the propagators—rats, the
unsuspected and therefore invulnerable culprits?

When its causes were discovered, the plague came to be

looked upon merely as one of the many infectious diseases
that continually threaten man's health and that abound in
unsanitary environments. Not knowing this, medieval popu-
lations lived in extremely unhygienic surroundings and
barely bothered about them. They made their way through
filth, which littered the public thoroughfares, slept in dark,
unventilated rooms, had no water to bathe in, and avoided
sunlight. These conditions provided extremely favorable
breeding grounds not only for the plague, but for countless
other diseases that ran rampant. They were less apparent in
their manifestations, because they only attacked individuals
or families and did not interfere with the daily life of a large
part of mankind.

When the means were found to fight the plague, all the
other infectious diseases could be tackled by taking the basic
step necessary for the prevention of all disease: cleaning up
people's public and private surroundings, both their cities
and their homes. The fight against the plague was the first
chapter in the story of man's protecting himself against the
minute, invisible living creatures that threaten his existence.

But personal hygiene, which was the end result of this long
battle, is based on quite a different fundamental concept:
man's personal health becomes the most important factor,
because the individual in perfect health, with a strong, well-
developed body, can be exposed to disease germs and not be
infected. Personal health is closely related to man's mastery of
himself and to the reverence shown to life and all its natural
beauties. The aim became not so much to fight against
disease as to attain health, thus shielding oneself against
disease in general. This was a new idea, and when it was first
propounded man was not a healthy creature. He was either
overfed or underfed, and he was full of poisons, or rather was
an inveterate self-poisoner. He delighted in killing himself or

causing himself pain. He was fond of overeating, of poisoning himself with alcohol, of lounging about doing nothing. It was his pleasure and his privilege to refuse the healing gifts of nature—the sun, the fresh air, exercise. The most surprising revelation brought about by this new concept of hygiene was not the fact that there were dangers connected with malnutrition and poverty in general; these dangers had been recognized and had been a matter of concern since the Middle Ages, or rather, since antiquity. The real revelation was the fact that the things that people greatly enjoyed and sought out as a coveted privilege were also harbingers of death. Giving up rich, heavy meals that lasted for hours, exquisite and tempting vintages, or a life of indolence had been considered a sacrifice, a penance, not a road to good health. It represented the renunciation of immediate gratification, the sacrificing of the pleasures of life. But underlying this kind of gratification was a degradation people were not even aware of: it was the gratification of men who were prey to sloth, who had lost their vital energies. The hosts of microorganisms attacked people who were already weak and perhaps even dying. But when man's taste for life was reborn and prevailed once again, people began to fear the consequences of their weaknesses and indulgences. They hastened out into the sunlight and became physically active with a feeling of joyous liberation. The simple life—eating only as much as necessary and no more, choosing a diet of fruits, vegetables and even raw food, taking exercise, plunging into life-restoring, natural activities—has become the goal of modern pleasure-seekers, those who want to live a long life and conquer disease.

The concept of personal hygiene has thus completely reversed the old values; that is, the gratifications of what was once a race toward death have been given up for the gratifi-

cations of a race toward life. A saint of bygone days would
have looked upon the outer forms of such an existence as
implying an effort at perfect penance.

In the area of morality, however, there has not been a
single step forward, and we are as backward in this respect as
people in the Middle Ages were with respect to hygiene. The
fact that there are unknown menaces to our moral lives is totally ignored, and only the most superficial changes are taken
into consideration: the fact that morals are less strict today is
taken to be a form of modern freedom, a fight against age-old
moral restrictions that had remained unchanged since the
days when leading a healthy life was regarded as the greatest
of sacrifices. Working less and allowing machines to do our
labor for us is the greatest goal of the contemporary era. And
underlying this chaotic moral life is an overweening ambition to acquire a great deal of money, an ambition that be-
trays the existence of that irresistible vice that goes by the
name of greed—a vice that is the equivalent in the moral
sphere of sloth in the physical sphere, for both represent a
form of hoarding and illusory enjoyment. But man declines,
for this sort of enjoyment is rooted in two vices—the wide
world that would open out and challenge him were he to live
a healthy life remains hidden to him, and he unconsciously
isolates himself, consumes himself in the dark shadows of unsatisfied pleasure-seeking. If we were to search for an analogy
with pathology in this domain, too, this moral situation
might be compared to the hidden, life-threatening ravages of
tuberculosis. In its beginning stages tuberculosis rouses its
victims to engage in a frantic pursuit of pleasure, though the
presence of the disease may remain unsuspected and unde-
tected for a long time. Thus the plague represents a sudden,
catastrophic scourge, and tuberculosis represents the gradual
self-destruction of the weak personality.

14   Foundations for Peace

We live, in short, in a state of moral paralysis, in dark and suffocating shadows, and often we allow ourselves collectively to be carried away by statements that feed our illusions. Ever so many moralists continually say that our error today lies in wanting to base everything on man's reason, and as many others are convinced that progress cannot be based solely on man's reason and its dictatorial claims to rule our entire lives. But each side is quite certain that reason is sovereign and triumphant today. The truth of the matter, however, is that reason today is hidden under a dark cloud and has almost gone down to defeat. Moral chaos in fact is nothing but one side of the coin of our psychic decline; the other side is the loss of our powers of reason. The preeminent characteristic of our present state is an insidious madness, and our most immediate need a return to reason.

The battle between adult and child

In order to begin the task of reconstructing man's psyche, we must make the child our point of departure. We must recognize that he is more than just our progeny, more than just a creature who is our greatest responsibility. We must study him not as a dependent creature, but as an independent person who must be considered in terms of his own individual self. We must have faith in the child as a messiah, as a savior capable of regenerating the human race and society. We must master ourselves and humble ourselves in order to be able to accept this notion, and then we must make our way toward the child, like the three kings, bearing powers and gifts, following the star of hope.

Rousseau sought to discover in the child man's pure and natural characteristics before they are sidetracked and spoiled by the influence of society. This is a challenging theoretical problem, and thanks to a fertile effort of imagination Rousseau was able to build an entire novel around it. Were a psychologist to deal with the subject in the abstract, he would doubtless view it in terms of an embryology of the human mind.

But when we for our part studied the newborn child, who turned out to have unsuspected and surprising psychic characteristics, we found something more than an embryonic mind. We were deeply moved at the discovery of a real and awesome conflict, a ceaseless war, that confronts the child from the very day he is born and is part of his life all during his formative years. This conflict is between the adult and the child, between the strong and the weak, and, we might add, between the blind and the clearsighted.

The adult is truly blind to the child, and the child has real vision, a bright little flame of enlightenment that he brings us as a gift. Both the adult and the child are unaware of their own characteristic natures. They fight one another in a secret struggle that has gone on for countless generations and is becoming even more violent today in our complicated and nerve-racking culture. The adult defeats the child; and once the child reaches adulthood the characteristic signs of the peace that is only an aftermath of war—destruction on one hand and painful adjustment on the other—remain with him for the rest of his life.

The child for his part cannot lift up the fallen older man by lending him his own fresh strength and life-renewing vitality, because the adult becomes an adversary whose first gesture is to stifle him.

This situation is much more serious today than at any time in the past. By constructing an environment that is further and further removed from nature, and thus more and more unsuited to a child, the adult has increased his own powers and thereby tightened his hold over the child. No new moral

sensibility has made its appearance to free the adult from the
selfishness that blinds him, and no new understanding of the
many changes in the human situation that are unfavorable to
children has penetrated the minds of mature human beings.
The age-old, superficial notion that the development of the
individual is uniform and progressive remains unchanged,
and the mistaken idea that the adult must mold the child in
the pattern that society wishes still holds sway. This gross,
time-hallowed misconception is the source of the primary
conflict, even war, between human beings who by all rights
should love and cherish one another—parents and children,
teachers and pupils.

The key to this problem lies in the two different forms and
goals of the human personality—one of which is characteristic of children and the other of adults. The child is not
simply a miniature adult. He is first and foremost the pos-
sessor of a life of his own that has certain special characteristics and that has its own goal. The child's goal might be
summed up in the word *incarnation;* the incarnation of
human individuality must take place within him.

The child's work, aimed entirely at this incarnation, has
vital characteristics and rhythms that are totally different
from the adult's. That is why the latter is the great trans-
former of the environment and the social being par excellence.

If we think for a moment of the embryo, we may perhaps
understand this concept more clearly. The one aim of the
embryo within the womb is to attain the maturity of the newborn child. This constitutes the prenatal phase of man's life.
The most vigorous newborn child will be the one who has developed in the womb in the very best conditions that a
healthy mother can offer him, taking no special care other
than to allow the new creature to live within her.

But man's later gestation is not as brief as the one in his

mother's womb. The child goes through another kind of gestation in the outside world, incarnating a spirit whose seeds are latent and unconscious within him.

Delicate care is required to protect the child as he does his work, of which he becomes conscious little by little and which he performs by means of experiences in contact with the outside world. The child performs work with inner wisdom, guided by laws like those that guide every other task that is accomplished in the realm of nature, following rhythms of activity that do not have the slightest resemblance to those of the aggressive adult bent on conquest.

The concept of the work of incarnation or spiritual gestation as being completely different from the labors of the adult human active in the social order is not a new one. On the contrary, it has been solemnly and eloquently celebrated for many centuries and comes down to us with all the force of a sacred rite. There are two holidays in the year that all of us observe—Christmas and Easter. We celebrate them in our hearts and take time off from our social labors, and many of us attend religious services on these two occasions. What do these age-old holidays commemorate? One single Person. But the incarnation and the social mission of this Person are recognized separately and distinctly.

In the story of the life of Jesus, his incarnation lasts until puberty, until approximately the age of thirteen, when the young boy says to his elders, "How is it that ye sought me? Wist ye not that I must be about my Father's business?" This is a young boy speaking. He has not learned wisdom from adults, but rather, amazes and confounds them. Only later do we learn of the obscure life of the boy who obeyed his elders, who did his best to learn his father's trade, and who came in contact with the society of men in which he was to fulfill his mission.

Let us suppose now that the characteristics and goals of the independent life of childhood are not recognized and that the adult takes those characteristics that are different from his own to be mistakes on the part of the child and hastens to correct them. At this point a battle will take place between the weaker and the stronger that is crucial for humanity, because the sickness or health of man's soul, his strength or weakness of character, the clear light or dark shadows of his mind depend on whether or not the child has a tranquil and perfect spiritual life.

And if in this delicate and precious period of life a sacrilegious form of enslavement of the child is practiced, the seeds of life will become sterile, and it will no longer be possible for men to carry out the great works that life has summoned them to perform.

Now the battle between adults and children takes place in the family and in the school, during the process that is still referred to by the time-hallowed word *education*.

When we took the personality of the child into account in and of itself and offered it full scope to develop in our schools —where we constructed an environment that answered the needs of his spiritual development—he revealed to us a personality entirely different from the one we had previously taken into consideration, with traits exactly the opposite of those attributed to him by others. With his passionate love of order and work, the child gave evidence of intellectual powers vastly superior to what they were presumed to be. It is obvious that in traditional systems of education the child instinctively resorts to dissemblance in order to conceal his capabilities and conform to the expectations of the adults who suppress him.

The child bows to the cruel necessity of hiding himself, burying in his subconscious a life force that cries out to express itself and that is fatally frustrated. Bearing as he does this hidden burden, he, too, will eventually perpetuate mankind's many errors.

The question of the relationship of education to war and peace lies therein, rather than in the content of the culture passed on to the child. Whether or not the problem of war is discussed with children, whether or not the history of mankind is presented in this or that form to children in no way changes the fate of human society.

The failure, the weakling, the slave, and the arrested personality are, in short, always the products of an education that is a blind struggle between the strong and the weak.

The fact that the child has character traits quite different from those he was long believed to possess has been proved incontrovertibly after a quarter of a century of constant work, not only in almost every nation that shares our Western heritage, but also among many other widely divergent ethnic groups: American Indians, Africans, Siamese, Javanese, Laplanders. After our initial experiences, there was enthusiastic talk of a method of education capable of producing astonishing results, but soon thereafter many people became aware of the reality and the importance of this phenomenon. One of the first books on the subject, entitled *New Children*,[1] was published in England.

We have had a glimpse of a new kind of humanity aborning. There was awakened the hope of better men, the hope of eliminating the deviations that cripple children in their formative years, replacing them with a normal process of development, and allowing man to attain psychic health at last.

The man with a sound psyche is such a rare creature today that we almost never meet one, just as men with sound bodies

[1]Sheila Radice, *New Children* (Frederick A. Stokes & Co., 1920).

were few and far between before the concept of personal
hygiene helped mankind recognize the basis of physical
health. In the moral domain man still finds pleasure in subtle
poisons and covets privileges that conceal mortal perils for
the spirit. What are often called virtue, duty, and honor are
no more than masks for capital vices that education passes on
from generation to generation. The child's unsatisfied aspirations have an effect on him as an adult and betray themselves
in different expressions of arrested mental development, in
moral defects, in countless psychic anomalies that cause the
human personality to become weak and unstable.

The child who has never learned to work by himself, to set
goals for his own acts, or to be the master of his own force of
will is recognizable in the adult who lets others guide him
and feels a constant need for the approval of others.

The schoolchild who is continually discouraged and repressed comes to lack confidence in himself. He suffers from a
sense of panic that goes by the name of timidity, a lack of self-
assurance that in the adult takes the form of frustration and
submissiveness and the inability to resist what is morally
wrong. The obedience forced upon a child at home and in
school, an obedience that does not recognize the rights of
reason and justice, prepares the adult to resign himself to
anything and everything. The widespread practice in educational institutions of exposing a child who makes mistakes to
public disapproval, and indeed to a sort of public pillorying,
instills in him an uncontrollable and irrational terror of
public opinion, however unfair and erroneous that opinion
may be. And through these and many other kinds of condi-
tioning that lead to a sense of inferiority, the way is opened
to the spirit of unthinking respect, and indeed almost
mindless idolatry, in the minds of paralyzed adults toward
public leaders, who come to represent surrogate teachers and

fathers, figures upon whom the child was forced to look as perfect and infallible. And discipline thus becomes almost synonymous with slavery.

The child thus far has been deprived of the possibility of venturing on moral paths that his latent vital impulses might have sought anxiously in a world that is completely new to him. He never has been able to measure and test his own creative energies; he never has been able to establish the sort of inner order whose primary consequence is a confident and inviolable sense of discipline.

The child's attempts to learn what real justice is have been confused and misdirected. He has even been punished for charitably having tried to help schoolmates who were more oppressed and less quick-witted than he. If, on the other hand, he spied on and denounced others, he met with tolerance. The most rewarded and most encouraged virtue has been besting his classmates and coming out on top, triumphantly passing examinations at the end of every year of his life of perpetual, monotonous slavery. Men educated in this manner have not been prepared to seek truth and to make it an intimate part of their lives, nor to be charitable toward others and to cooperate with them to create a better life for all. On the contrary, the education they have received has prepared them for what can be considered only an interlude in real collective life—war. For the truth of the matter is that war is caused not by arms but by man.

If man were to grow up fully and with a sound psyche, developing a strong character and a clear mind, he would be unable to tolerate the existence of diametrically opposed moral principles within himself or to advocate simultaneously two sorts of justice—one that fosters life and one that destroys it. He would not simultaneously cultivate two moral powers in his heart, love and hatred. Nor would he erect two disciplines, one that marshals human energies to build, another that marshals them to destroy what has been built. A strong man cannot stand a split within his consciousness, much less act in two exactly opposite ways. Thus if human reality is different from what it actually appears to be in everyday life, it is because men allow themselves to be passive and are blown this way and that like dead leaves.

War today does not stem from hating an enemy. How can it, when today men fight against one nation one day and another the next, and tomorrow's ally is yesterday's enemy? The white man who boasts of being a highly civilized creature is no better morally than the mercenary armies of the past who would fight anybody, as long as they were paid. Nothing has changed, except perhaps the fact that today men destroy their own handiwork and treasures and suffer famine simply because they have been ordered to do so. The Egyptians were wise enough to make a distinction between the work of building their civilization and the waging of war. They therefore paid Phoenecian troops to fight their battles while their own people cultivated the land and engaged in public works projects. But we "civilized" nations confuse the two things.

Faced with the difficult social problems that cause such grave concern in our time, better men than we are would use their intelligence and their forefathers' hard-won victories in the battle to become civilized to find solutions other than war. Otherwise why should man be possessed of intelligence? And what point is there in our possessing the riches accumulated for us by the wisdom of our forefathers? For a better man, war would not even be a problem; it would simply be a barbarous practice diametrically opposed to civilized life, an absurdity completely beyond the comprehension of the new man. It is up to man to choose his fate, and the day

that his weapons fall from his hand will mark the beginning
of a radiant future for mankind.

The Third Dimension

It would seem to be so obvious a statement as to be naive,
but it is perfectly plain that two things are needed for peace
in the world: first of all, a new man, a better man; and then
an environment that henceforth will set no limits on man's
boundless aspirations.

It would be necessary for the sources of wealth to be
equally accessible to all rather than the patrimony of any one
country. How can we guarantee that the peoples of the world
will let others freely travel on the roads that they have built
and exploit the riches buried beneath the soil of their
country? In order to unite all men as brothers, we would
have to tear down all the barriers, so that human beings the
world over would be like children playing in one vast garden.
Laws and treaties are not enough; what is required is a new
world, full of miracles.

The child also seems to work miracles when we realize how
eagerly he seeks independence and the opportunity to work,
and he possesses great treasures of enthusiasm and love.

A new world for a new man—this is our most urgent need.
If this were a utopia, or some sort of joke, it would be a
sacrilege to speak of it at this moment when humanity is living on the edge of an abyss, threatened with total catastrophe.
But we have had blindingly vivid glimpses of a world of miracles since the beginning of this century.

Is it not true that man can now fly? As a result, geographical barriers no longer separate one country from another,
and man can go anywhere on earth without building roads
and without invading the territory of others.

And if man has managed to overcome the force of gravity

and to travel freely and swiftly in the air, what country will henceforth be able to insist on territorial rights to this or that part of the earth? What country will be able to claim exclusive rights over the gravity of the earth or the outer space beyond the earth's atmosphere? Who will have exclusive claim to the long waves and the short waves, the invisible causes of a mysterious kind of communication that nonetheless transports the voice of man and the thoughts of all humanity through space? And who can ever completely exhaust this great freedom and power?

Solar energy will be transformed into more nourishing bread and heat for men's dwellings. What nation will be able to claim exclusive rights over it? There are no limits, no geographical restrictions on the new riches that man is acquiring as he moves toward the stratosphere, toward the infinite heavens, toward the starry heart of creation. What point will there be then in a struggle of man with man?

Men first fought over concrete things, but then they discovered that the origin of material phenomena was energy. Thereafter man mastered the infinite, hidden causes rather than their limited effects. Man mastered them as if he were a god, and thereby completely changed his life as a social being. A marvelous, rapid conquest of the sphere above the earth has raised the conquests of man onto a level beyond its surface. The surface of the earth had two dimensions for man, but now he has moved toward the third dimension. The two-dimensional history of mankind is now ended.

An era that lasted for thousands of years, one as old as human history, beginning in fact in a legendary age and before that in epochs of which we have only a few traces buried in the bowels of the earth, has now come to an end. An immense chapter of history taking millennia to unfold has now closed.

Until our own time, man had to earn his daily bread by the sweat of his brow, cultivating the fields like a condemned man, and he had to hide his nobility like a slave. He, though the son of love, was forced to bear the chains of exchanges of material goods. But the man who has invaded the world of the stars can rise up in all his grandeur, can confront the universe as a new creature. The child, the new child, is predestined to march on to the conquest of the infinite.

This conquest is so vast in scope that it requires the cooperation of all mankind, but the one thing that will forge true human unity is love.

This is the vision of reality of our time: we, the last earthbound men, must make the great effort of lifting up our eyes and hearts to understand it. We are undergoing a crisis, torn between an old world that is coming to an end and a new world that has already begun and already given proof of all the constructive elements it has to offer. The crisis we are experiencing is not the sort of upheaval that marks the passage from one historical period to another. It can be compared only to one of those biological or geological epochs in which new, higher, more perfect forms of life appeared, as totally new conditions of existence on earth came about.

If we do not appreciate this situation for what it is, we shall find ourselves confronting a universal cataclysm, mindful of the prophecy of the Apocalypse. If man remains earthbound and unconscious of the new realities, if he uses the energies of space for the purpose of destroying himself, he will soon attain that goal, for the energies now at his disposal are immeasurable and accessible to everyone, at all times and in every corner of the earth.

And if man, who is privy to the secret of plagues and can control their causes and breed countless disease germs in his laboratories at will, uses this means of saving lives to spread

devastating epidemics that will poison the earth, he will accomplish his purpose with the greatest of ease.

There are no obstacles standing in his way today. Neither
mountains nor seas are a barrier, and he can reach the re-
motest corner of the earth by flying in the atmosphere.

Who will sound the trumpet awakening him? Man today
lies slumbering on the surface of the earth, which is about to
swallow him up. What will he do?

2 For Peace

Men with the best minds on earth gather today in answer to a call to solve life's most urgent problems.

Peace is a goal that can be attained only through common accord, and the means to achieve this unity for peace are twofold: first, an immediate effort to resolve conflicts without recourse to violence—in other words, to prevent war—and second, a long-term effort to establish a lasting peace among men. Preventing conflicts is the work of politics; establishing peace is the work of education. We must convince the world of the need for a universal, collective effort to build the foundation for peace.

Constructive education for peace must not be limited to the teaching in schools. It is a task that calls for the efforts of all mankind. It must aim to reform humanity so as to permit the inner development of human personality and to develop a more conscious vision of the mission of mankind and the present conditions of social life. These aims must be achieved not only because man is almost totally unaware of his own nature, but also because for the most part he does not understand the workings of the social mechanisms on which his interests and his immediate salvation depend.

This address was given before the European Congress for Peace in Brussels on September 3, 1936.

27

The most characteristic phenomenon of modern life is the sudden change in our social conditions. The outward change is obvious, for scientific discoveries and their practical applications have brought about amazing changes in our physical environment. But this change is perhaps not so apparent at deeper and more essential levels underlying these outward changes in our civilization. This second level on which change has occurred is proof nonetheless that thanks to economic mechanisms and communications, men have in fact managed to become united in their material interests.

This achievement indicates that new goals have emerged in the field of these interests themselves, and it is necessary that men be consciously educated to fulfill them, for if men continue to regard themselves as national groups with divergent interests, they will run the risk of destroying one another. This is the crux of all the questions regarding peace.

As a consequence of these changes, war is now pointless and cannot yield any material profit. The [first world] war in Europe has already shown that the victors have not gained new energies and benefits from their victory, as victors did in the past. An entirely new phenomenon has occurred: defeated peoples have become a danger, a burden, an obstacle. The victors must aid them and help them get back on their feet. A conquered nation today is an illness that all of mankind suffers. The impoverishment of one nation does not make another nation richer; rather, all nations decline. Destroying one nation is tantamount to cutting off one hand in the mistaken hope that the other hand will thereby become twice as strong.

We are all a single organism, one nation. By becoming a single nation we have finally realized the unconscious spiritual and religious aspiration of the human soul, and this we can proclaim to every corner of the earth. "Humanity as an organism" has been born; the superconstruction that has absorbed all man's efforts from the beginning of his history has now been completed. We are living this reality. We have proof of it in the almost miraculous powers that today are enabling man to rise above his natural condition. Man now flies higher and more confidently through the heavens than the eagle; he has mastered the invisible secrets of the energy of the universe; he can look up into the skies and the infinite; his voice can cross the world's seas, and he can hear the echoes of all the world's music; he now possesses the secret powers of transforming matter. In a word, contemporary man has citizenship in the great nation of humanity.

It is absurd to believe that such a man, endowed with powers superior to those of nature, should be a Dutchman or a Frenchman or an Englishman or an Italian. He is the new citizen of the new world—a citizen of the universe.

This being the case, it is no longer possible to assume the existence of nations with divergent interests. Separate nations with their own borders, their own customs, their own exclusive rights no longer have any reason for being. There will always be human groups and human families with different traditions and languages, but these cannot be sufficient reason for the existence of nations in the traditional sense of the word: they must unite as constituent elements of a single organism or die. The great trumpet calling men to rally around the one banner of humanity is a summons on which our very life depends. Today all men are in touch with one another; ideas circulate through the air by radio from one end of the earth to the other, recognizing no national boundaries; groups sharing the same ideas are being formed all over the world, and men can no longer cling to the medieval mentality of the Palleschi and Piagnoni in Italy.[1]

---

[1]These were the two parties for and against the Medici family in Florence.

Special-interest groups, however, are attempting today to take over these enormous powers that henceforth must belong to humanity as a whole.

There are only two paths before us: we must either prove worthy of our great achievements or die as a result of them. It is absurd to fight each other for material well-being or national defense or the triumph of one social system or another.

Our era is a time of adjustment to material conditions that have undergone vast changes. We have conquered our physical environment and overcome our purely natural limitations. We have mastered invisible powers and taken the place of the Jupiter Tonans of the Greeks and the gods of the Hellenic peoples. But we are not yet fully aware that we have done so, and this is precisely what prevents us from becoming brothers in order that this superworld may become the Kingdom of Heaven.

Man must be educated to realize his greatness and to become worthy of the powers that are his. If, in the Rome of the Empire, the Roman citizen needed to be aware of his dignity, it is even more necessary that today's citizen of the Universal Empire become aware of his.

The human personality has remained as it was in the conditions of the past: man's character and mentality have remained unchanged, and he does not understand the destiny and responsibility that he now has because of the new powers at his disposal. Man, in short, has not kept pace with the progress that has been made in his external environment; he remains timid and confused, fearful and susceptible to blind submission to authority, to a return to paganism or even barbarism, because he feels overwhelmed by the superworld in which he lives.

Modern psychologists have spoken of the dangers that threaten the individual who is a victim of a so-called inferiority complex; but what can we say of the perils that threaten all humanity because man, the king of the universe, trembles with fear and is so overcome with depression that he is tempted to do away with himself?

Our principal concern must be to educate humanity—the human beings of all nations—in order to guide it toward seeking common goals. We must turn back and make the child our principal concern. The efforts of science must be concentrated on him, because he is the source of and the key to the riddles of humanity. The child is richly endowed with powers, sensitivities, and constructive instincts that as yet have neither been recognized nor put to use. In order to develop, he needs much broader opportunities than he has been offered thus far. Might not this goal be reached by changing the entire structure of education? Society must fully recognize the social rights of the child and prepare for him and the adolescent a world capable of ensuring their spiritual development.

In order to do this, all nations would have to reach an understanding, to bring about a sort of truce that would permit each of them to devote itself to the cultivation of its own human members in order to find therein the practical solutions to social problems that today seem insuperable.

Perhaps the attainment of peace would then be easy and close at hand, like waking from a dream, like freeing ourselves from a hypnotic spell.

3 Educate for Peace

Education today, in this particular social period, is assuming truly unlimited importance. And the increased emphasis on its practical value can be summed up in one sentence: education is the best weapon for peace.

If we consider the awesome power and technical perfection of armaments, which people trust to protect them in war, we are forced to conclude that education will not become an armament capable of ensuring the security and progress of the peoples of the world until it has attained the same level of excellence and scientific development.

I am not speaking of the possible need for mechanical armaments, and I do not want to deal with the political question; I am merely saying that the true defense of mankind cannot be based on arms. Wars will always follow one upon the other, and no people's peace and prosperity can ever be assured until we trust in the great "armament for peace" that education represents.

Since education is the true salvation of humanity and civilization, it cannot be restricted to its present limits nor continue in its present form. Education today has fallen far behind contemporary needs. To use an analogy in keeping

This address was given in Copenhagen on May 22, 1937.

with the subject at hand, it might be said that education has
remained at the level of the bow and arrow in comparison
with today's armaments. How can we fight powerful cannons
and aerial bombardments with bows and arrows? That is why
it is necessary to build and perfect the armament of education.

It is obvious that education as the cornerstone of peace
cannot consist only in attempting to prevent children from
becoming fascinated by war. It is not enough to keep the
child from playing with toy weapons, to stop making him
study the history of mankind as a succession of feats of arms,
and to stop teaching him that victory on the battlefield is a
supreme honor. It is not even enough to instill in the child a
love and a respect for all living beings and all the things that
human beings have built through the centuries.

This would be the role of the classroom in a much greater
task, a campaign against war in and of itself, a role that we
might describe as a negative one—the mere attempt to
remove the threat of an imminent conflict—rather than a
positive effort to bring about peace in the world.

It is all too obvious that wars cannot be prevented by an
education of this kind. If they could be, why have they not
been prevented by the educational influence of civilized society, which proclaims that man's life and liberty are sacred, or
by the influence of religions, which have tried for thousands
of years to teach man to love his fellows?

Men do not go off to war because they are bloodthirsty or
impatient to use their weapons. They would rather not fight
wars, but they are drawn into them. They are all terrified of
the scourge of war and would all like to escape it, and great
moral and material pressure must be applied to make them
abandon the safety of their homes and family life with their
loved ones.

Men do not fight wars because they played with toy weapons when they were children. And teaching history based on memorizing dates and events is certainly not the ideal method for making children want to be heroes.

War is clearly a complex phenomenon that we must investigate and understand, especially in our time. Humanity today is overwhelmed by events affecting the entire world with which education has not yet come to grips. Mankind today is like a small child who finds himself alone and lost in a forest, at the mercy of any shadow that falls across his path and of any mysterious noise heard in the dark.

Man does not understand the events that overwhelm him and is totally unable to protect himself against them. Society has evolved in a purely external way, constructing enormous mechanisms and setting up complicated means of communication, but humanity meanwhile has remained ignorant and disorganized. Yes, the world's peoples are disorganized, and each individual thinks only of his own immediate well-being.

Education as it is commonly regarded encourages individuals to go their own way and pursue their own personal interests. Schoolchildren are taught not to help one another, not to prompt their classmates who don't know the answers, but to concern themselves only with getting promoted at the end of the year and to win prizes in competition with fellow pupils. And these poor, selfish little creatures, who experimental psychology has proved are mentally exhausted, find themselves in later life like separate grains of sand in the desert; each one is isolated from his neighbor, and all of them are barren. If a storm comes up, these little human particles possessed of no life-giving spirituality are caught up in the gusts and form a deadly whirlwind.

An education capable of saving humanity is no small undertaking; it involves the spiritual development of man, the enhancement of his value as an individual, and the preparation of young people to understand the times in which they live.

The secret is this: making it possible for man to become the master of the mechanical environment that oppresses him today. Man the producer must become the master of production. Production today has been intensified by science and has become highly organized all over the world. It has therefore become necessary both to enhance human energies scientifically and to organize humanity proportionately. Men can no longer remain ignorant of their own natures and the world in which they live. The real scourge that threatens them today is precisely this sort of ignorance. We must organize our efforts for peace and prepare the way for it scientifically, through education. Education points the way to a new world to conquer: the world of the human spirit.

In our experience with children, we observed that the human child is a spiritual embryo, endowed with mysterious sensitivities that guide him, with creative energies that tend to construct a sort of marvelous instrument in men's souls. Like a radio set that can receive the long and short waves that are transmitted through space, the sort of instrument that a child gradually constructs in his own soul is destined to receive the holy waves transmitting divine love through the boundless spheres of eternity. It is this sensitivity that makes man uniquely valuable: man is great because he can receive the emanations of the Godhead.

The child is also capable of developing and giving us tangible proof of the possibility of a better humanity. He has shown us the true process of construction of the normal human being. We have seen children totally change as they acquire a love for things and as their sense of order, discipline, and self-control develops within them as a manifestation of their total freedom. We have seen them labor steadily, drawing on their own energies and developing them as they work.

The child is both a hope and a promise for mankind. If we therefore mind this embryo as our most precious treasure, we will be working for the greatness of humanity. The men we educate in this way will be able to use divine powers to outstrip the men of today who have entrusted their fate to machines. What is needed is faith in the grandeur and superiority of man. If he has managed to master the cosmic energies circulating in the atmosphere, he will be able to understand that the fire of genius, the value of intelligence, the light of conscience are also energies to be organized, to be regulated, to be treasured and put to good use in human social life.

Today these energies are scattered; or, rather, they are repressed and misdirected through the errors perpetuated by a kind of education that still holds sway all over the world. The adult does not understand the child. Parents unconsciously battle with their children rather than helping them in their divine mission. Fathers and sons do not understand each other. An abyss yawns between them from the day the child is born. And this lack of understanding is man's undoing; it leads him astray, sickens his spirit, impoverishes him, and makes him fail to realize his potential. The lack of understanding between children and adults precipitates the tragedy of the human heart, which in later life manifests itself in a lack of sensitivity, in sloth, and in criminality. Those who have been humiliated are ashamed of themselves; the timid withdraw into their shells; the fearful seek their own personal comfort. All the potential wealth of man's personality comes to nothing.

Education must take advantage of the value of the hidden instincts that guide man as he builds his own life. Powerful among these instincts is the social drive. It has been our experience that if the child and the adolescent do not have a

chance to engage in a true social life, they do not develop a
sense of discipline and morality. These gifts in their case
become end products of coercion rather than manifestations
of freedom. The human personality is shaped by continuous
experiences; it is up to us to create for children, for adolescents, for young people an environment, a world that will
readily permit such formative experiences. The youngster's
personality must come in contact with the world of production after an apprenticeship in experience; man must be
guided first and foremost toward an awareness of his responsibilities with regard to human social organization. Thus from
early childhood on, human beings must have practical experience of what association is, and only then gradually fathom
the secrets of the technical evolution of this society.

Today we have an organization of machines. What is
needed are men capable of using machines to carry out a lofty
mission that each of them will be aware of and feel responsible for.

It is absolutely certain that the secret of future human
power lies hidden within humanity as it develops—within
young people.

Those nations that want war have managed to recognize
and give scope to the powers hidden in children and young
people to further their own interests, to organize them
socially, to make them an active force in society. It is a tragedy that this truth has thus far been recognized only by those
powers that seek war. But the fact that a truly powerful organization of humanity cannot be improvised overnight is a reality that has great practical value. The groundwork for such
an organization must be laid in childhood, at the very roots
of life. Society can be organized, in short, only if education
offers man a ladder of social experiences as he passes from one
period of his life to another.

Those who want war prepare young people for war; but

those who want peace have neglected young children and adolescents, for they have been unable to organize them for peace.

Peace is a practical principle of human civilization and social organization that is based on the very nature of man. Peace does not enslave him; rather, it exalts him. It does not humiliate him, but rather makes him conscious of his own power over the universe. And because it is based on man's nature, it is a constant, a universal principle that applies to all human beings.

This principle must be our guide in building a science of peace and educating men for peace.

II

Educate for Peace, Sixth International Montessori Congress

4 Address Opening the Congress

This solemn ceremony today in the presence of Your Excellency, the minister of education of Denmark, marks the opening of our Sixth International Congress. This is not a pedagogical congress in the narrow sense of the word. The purpose of our congresses is to defend the child. The goal we have therefore set ourselves is to help the adult world know, love, and serve the child better, thereby helping all mankind reach a higher stage of development.

The child should not be regarded as a feeble and helpless creature whose only need is to be protected and helped, but as a spiritual embryo, possessed of an active psychic life from the day that he is born and guided by subtle instincts enabling him to actively build up the human personality. And since it is the child who becomes the adult man, we must consider him as the true builder of mankind and recognize him as our father. The great secret of our origin lies hidden within him, and the laws that will lead man to his rightful state of being can be manifested only within him. In this sense the child is our teacher. Adults must above all be educated to acknowledge this fact so that they may change

The following series of addresses was given at the Sixth International Montessori Congress in Copenhagen in 1937.

41

their behavior toward the generations that come after them.

By considering the child as a passive *tabula rasa,* without inner directives, the adult has in fact forced him to bend to the will of his elders and adapt to the conditions of the adult world. The adult has thus repressed the child's sensitive natural inclinations and trampled them underfoot, rousing in him unconquerable instinctive resistances and defenses capable of degenerating into real spiritual illnesses.

Man's life thus begins with an unconscious battle between the adult and the child; and as one generation follows another, man continues to be not a well-developed being but a deformed one, a person far from the ideal of the normal man with a personality balanced in its intellectual and affective aspects.

Society must recognize the importance of the child as the builder of humanity and come to have a profound appreciation of the psychic roots determining whether the mature adult will seek positive or negative goals. The child today is a "forgotten citizen"; society must now turn its attention to him and create an environment that will fulfill his vital needs and foster his spiritual liberation.

A great social mission that will ensure the child justice, harmony, and love remains to be accomplished. And this great task must be the work of education, for this is the only way to build a new world and to bring peace.

Bringing up the subject of an education for peace in such critical times as these, when society is continually threatened by the possibility of war, may appear to be a most naive kind of idealism. I nonetheless believe that laying the foundations for peace through education is the most effective and the most constructive way of opposing war, since peoples' needs today in no way justify armed combat, and since war offers them no hope whatsoever of bettering their lot.

Humanity has fallen into such a state of barbarism and spiritual disorganization that the individual has become nothing more than a tiny grain of sand in an arid desert. Each individual remains unaware of the true face of his own time and has no idea of the dangers that lie concealed within it until he becomes a helpless victim of events.

Given such a state of affairs, there can be no progress nor any hope for peace until swift and forceful action is taken and directed toward mankind itself.

Directing our action toward mankind means, first and foremost, doing so with regard to the child. The child, that "forgotten citizen," must be appreciated in accordance with his true value. His rights as a human being who shapes all of mankind must become sacred, and the secret laws of his normal psychic development must light the way for civilization.

If the era in the history of human evolution that is characterized by the constant outbreak of war can be called the "adult period," then the period in which we will begin to build peace will be the "age of the child."

As the law of brute force triumphed in the past, so today the laws of life must triumph. This extremely complex aspiration is best summarized by the word *education*.

Your Excellency, the generous hospitality offered our Sixth Congress by the Government of Denmark is a promising presage of peace for us and the world; for Denmark today, as always in the past, worships peace and the treasures of the human intellect.

Denmark stands ready to consider the problem of the child and to promote education as the primary tool for building peace. I should like to add that our first conference on the problem of the child was also held in Denmark, eight years ago—in Elsinore, near the royal castle whose legend inspired

Shakespeare. When the war in Europe ended, there was every hope of peace, and we defenders of the child chose as our meeting place the homeland of that genius of letters, Hans Christian Andersen, whose books have delighted children the world over. But war did not become a thing of the past, because wars will end only when humanity undergoes a spiritual reconstruction.

Our appeal to the world to realize the importance of the child in the spiritual development of mankind flies in the face of all intellectual movements whose interests are centered solely on adults. We are therefore all the more grateful to those who have come here to lend us their official support. We are honored that many public figures and governments are collaborating with us and that participants from twenty-five nations have gathered here for this congress, summoned by the still feeble call of the child, which has only recently begun to be heard in the world. In the name of our International Association, I wish to express thanks to my colleague Wilhelm Rasmussen, the director of the Institute for Advanced Teacher Training in Copenhagen, who generously assumed the task of organizing this congress.

Your Excellency, I wish to express my sincerest thanks to you for having given us your official support from the very beginning. And I would also like to express my profound gratitude to Their Excellencies Prime Minister Stauning and the minister of social affairs, Ludvig Christensen, who agreed to sponsor the organization of the congress as honorary presidents; and to His Excellency Dr. Munch, the minister of foreign affairs, who will pay this congress the honor of addressing it personally. Speaking on behalf of children everywhere, I wish to say, from the bottom of my heart: "Long live Denmark and the noble and generous hospitality it has offered the cause of peace in the world!"

Many governments are supporting this congress, the subject of which is almost a command: "Educate for peace!" Belgium, Catalonia, Chile, Czechoslovakia, France, Greece, Haiti, the Canton of Ticino, Latvia, Mexico, Rumania, Russia, the United States of America, and Egypt either have sent official representatives, or their diplomatic representatives in this capital have honored us by attending personally the opening of our congress.

5 Why May Education Have an Influence on the World Today?

The subject I have been asked to discuss today has a special significance because it presents itself in the form of a question: Why may education have an influence on the world today?

This way of formulating the question implies that education has not had such an influence at all times and in all circumstances. As a matter of fact, if education in and of itself is so strong an influence as to be able to oppose effectively the mobilization of powerful armies, for example, why has it not had such an effect in the past? For thousands of years Christianity and, before it, the great philosophies of antiquity have appealed to the feelings of love and brotherhood buried in the human soul. Yet men have continued to fight as if driven by an implacable force, in a struggle not unlike that described by Darwin between species. And perhaps there are those who will say that this is the way things have always been and always will be.

But today there exist such unprecedented new phenomena and such unusual forms of human warfare that we have good reason to believe that the entire course of past history unfolded on quite a different plane from that of history in our own era. If we study past wars, we see that they were the result of man's crucial needs to conquer others and to defend himself and that although other solutions to mankind's problems may have been possible, these wars brought certain advantages to one side at the expense of the other. What is more, such wars pitted one civilization against another and therefore were very effective means of selection. At times they also effected an important intermixture of peoples and a spreading of civilization, even though such results, as I said, might also have come about without war.

But today we are unable to perceive any positive advantages to war. Some people might object that the conquest of another nation constitutes an advantage. But we may well question whether this is true. Denmark has reached a high level of civilization without, in recent times, feeling the need to conquer other peoples. And why should it feel such a need? In order to gain a better food supply perhaps? But to do that, all a nation need do is buy and produce better foodstuffs on its own. Or perhaps to foster cultural progress by acquiring better means of transportation? But to do that all a nation need do is buy and construct. There is nothing anywhere in the world that cannot be produced and put to use. It seems evident to me that it would be easier to live without so many anxieties and to procure needed products from their places of origin than it is to conquer others and acquire material goods by force. Or perhaps nations resort to war to appropriate and exploit the discoveries of some genius who has lived in the conquered country? But there is no discovery—not even the most minor intellectual advance—in any corner of the world that does not soon become known from one end of the earth to the other, like liquid in connecting vessels that seeks a common level. So the age-old reasons no longer hold. One striking fact remains, however: an evolution of the social environment has come about, especially in the last few years —a sudden, miraculous evolution that we owe to just a handful of men. Their names I need not mention since the important thing is that they represent the forces of intelligence—that great energy, that immeasurable treasure that can bring benefits to the entire world even though it may shine forth in a single individual.

But all the discoveries and all the inventions that we appear to owe to a single individual depend on an ever-present, obscure substratum of workers who create a product that no one can conquer and appropriate by force. This labor is the patrimony of no one nation; it is more or less common to all of them. It is a supernatural stratum, which has created a supernatural world, a civilization that has spread everywhere.

Society has been transformed through these prodigious achievements; and we are not even conscious of this change, for it is the characteristic feature of our era. Man's impressive power to overcome the force of gravity and his power over elements once inaccessible to him are the distinctive mark of our time.

All men, moreover, have become richer. I would even go so far as to say that they are so rich that they are the victims of their wealth. If we compare our era with the past, we might say that this is the age of the rich. All our homes have water and light; all men have means of transportation at their disposal. How fortunate humanity is to have reached such a high level of universal wealth! Yes, humanity is so rich that man would like to return to a simpler way of life. He feels the need to resort to remedies that once were considered a penance: many people today consider it highly desirable to eat simply and live outdoors in a tent.

We have a great deal of monetary wealth as well. But even though people are seeking a way of life that in certain respects is healthier and simpler, they are used to their comforts and would not care to give them up. We might well be preaching to deaf ears were we to advocate giving up the outward forms of civilized life. No one will deny that the things we enjoy today—new means of transportation, electricity, radios, and the like—represent a very valuable form of progress.

One might suggest to a contemporary man, "Look at the sort of civilization that produced Demosthenes and Cicero and other great figures of the past who had an intense spiritual life. Let us live as they did then; let us give up the achievements of our civilization; let us give up electric lights!" He would object; no one would want to go back to the old days. Everyone would consider such a sacrifice rather silly. And if it were suggested, "Let us give up our bathrooms with running water and draw our water from wells," everyone would object, "But that has nothing to do with progress!" And someone might say, finally, "Friends, it is better to do away with all the new means of transportation—airplanes, automobiles, streetcars. Let us get about on foot or on horseback. If we return to these modes of transportation we will become nobler people!" Everyone would consider such preaching absurd. For we have come to realize that intellectual progress is not at odds with technical progress, but rather goes hand and hand with it. I am quite certain that if a heroic Franciscan possessed of a will of iron were to devote himself to preaching such a message, he would not win disciples today.

How has it happened that our level of human morality represents a step backward along the road to civilization? If someone preaches the need to kill others, why does everyone become his follower? Why are we urged to be heroes, just as in the past, without our ideas about heroism having changed in the slightest? We for our part will answer: humanity has made great progress outwardly, but none whatsoever inwardly. Man is totally unaware of one entire aspect of the problems confronting him. Nothing has been done to further his spiritual development. His personality has remained exactly the same as in past centuries, but the many changes that have occurred in his social conditions force him to live in an unnatural environment today. Man is thus weak and helpless in the face of the suggestions exercised both by his physical environment and by other men. He has no confidence in his judgment, and his personality is fragmented. This is what contemporary man is like, to put it kindly. Those who have made scientific studies of him have used much harsher words. They tell us that man's desperate struggle to adapt to his environment without being prepared to do so brings about changes in his personality that might be described as pathological. This is the most interesting problem of our time: all of us today feel gratified to be a little bit abnormal.

Statistics prove that our mental institutions, our hospitals for nervous diseases are full to overflowing, and that almost everyone at some time in his life needs to consult a specialist in mental illnesses, if only to be aware that he is suffering from one.

Even though we are not the only ones to have realized that some children thought to be normal actually are not, we were the *first* to be aware of this fact and the first to realize that this psychic scourge is even more devastating now than in the past, because the child today finds himself in an unprecedented postion. His situation cannot be described briefly. We must limit ourselves here to pointing out that there is no room for the child in the contemporary world. The child's world has come to be like a cone that is continually shrinking in size, leaving no place for him. What I mean by saying that there is no room in the world for the child is that there is neither physical space for him nor room for him in the minds and hearts of men. Mankind creates its own laws, and it evolves. And conditions for the child are worsening as conditions for the adult are improving. Even parents appear to be neglecting their children, because they have too much to do. And mankind, today so feeble, so sick, the victim of so many temptations, no longer has the strength to change its course. Humanity itself is thus the most important problem of our time.

The imbalance between the development of the external environment and man's inner spiritual development is quite striking. It is a curious phenomenon, one even more fraught with contradictions that the phenomenon of war. Men have achieved so much and could be so rich, and yet they are poor and unhappy. At this very moment everyone is asking how he can go on living. Everything is evolving, everything is changing, mankind is producing so much—indeed, too much—and it is this very excess that sometimes makes us want desperately to return to the past.

Enormous confusion reigns in the world! Contemporary man, that stunted homunculus, is full of contradictions. He does not even know whether he is rich or poor, sick or healthy. He is the victim of anxieties, of an anguish typical of a person who is seriously ill. He wonders how he can carry on. "How can I possibly manage?" is the phrase everyone gasps, in this marvelous world full of resources and new ways of life. Man is ready to sacrifice everything for this anguish-ridden end, which bears a striking resemblance to the anxiety of patients suffering from pathological neuroses. The men of antiquity were simpler. They said, God will provide. In their world there was still room for the poor man among others who were poor, and the individual was ready to make sacrifices for the good of one of his fellows. Today our anxieties about life are something like the desperate attempt to get out of a burning building alive. Man is ready and willing to give up almost anything, even his conscience, even his principles; he is ready and willing to give up his civilized humanity if only such a step will allow him to go on living.

Look at what has happened to the sort of education provided by parents and teachers! They tell the child, "Come on. You must buckle down and study. You must get that diploma. You must get such and such a job. Otherwise how will you live?" Parents and teachers today forget to voice the words that were once the very cornerstone of education: "All men are brothers."

The men of our times go through life dried up and isolated one from the other. Such dried and isolated men, even if they move about together, cannot form a real society, certainly not a fertile society in the midst of which moral progress and human uplift can thrive. Such men are like grains of sand in the desert. They are massed together, but they remain separate. The soil of their social life is sterile; even a light breeze can blow it about and ruin it. A little spiritual water would suffice to turn it into a stronger and less arid ground. Only a little life need grow there to bring about a beneficial change, because it is life that changes sand into fertile soil. The real threat that weighs on mankind today is not war so much as this desperate aridity, this arrest of development. The unhappiness of man is the most fearful feature of the reality of our times. He no longer feels any genuine joy. He is terrified. He feels himself inferior because of something within himself. He hides an emptiness within himself! And nature abhors a void. She yearns to fill it somehow.

The real danger threatening humanity is the emptiness in men's souls; all the rest is merely a consequence of this emptiness.

It is significant that in this age of progress man has discovered within himself that form of moral sickness that goes by the name of an inferiority complex. Man, the creature who flies through the heavens, who captures the music of the spheres, who is possessed of a power bordering on omnipotence, complains of being weak, ineffectual, and unhappy.

The fundamental problem is to cure humanity and take the noble concept of man as king of the universe as the lodestar of the development of human individuality. This human being who has harnessed every kind of physical power must now tame and tap his own inner powers, become the master of himself and the ruler of his own period of history. In order to do so, the value of individuality must be released and put to use. Its power must be experienced. Man must be taught to see the world in all its grandeur, to extend the limits of his life, to make his individual personality reach out and touch those of others.

The king of the universe, the king of heaven and earth, the king of visible objects and invisible energies—that is the sort of man who must rule! The whole earth is doubtless his domain, but his true kingdom is the one within himself.

I will conclude with a parable, which may seem quite humble, but nonetheless may shed light on what I have said thus far.

Let us imagine a prince who has a magnificent palace, full of superb works of art, Oriental rugs, precious objects, and so on. This prince marries a simple woman of the people. The good woman comes to live in the palace as a princess, but she walks over the splendid carpets without realizing their value, and she does not appreciate or admire the works of art. The prince then realizes that it is not enough simply to marry a woman of the people to make her a true princess; she must also be educated. He sees to it that she receives an education, and the woman then returns to the palace as a princess and enjoys the things that fate has put into her hands.

The civilized world is like the prince's palace, and mankind is like the woman of the people. The princess must be educated. This is the real problem—nothing else is really needed. The palace, dignity, a title are all at hand; the only thing lacking is education.

Education is enormously important today, because man possesses much more than he knows and much more than he can enjoy. He has everything! He must learn to appreciate what he has, to enjoy what he already possesses.

6   Second Lecture

I would like to propound an idea of fundamental importance: the sort of education required to advance the cause of
peace must necessarily be complex and altogether different
from what is ordinarily meant by the word *education*.

Education as it is ordinarily regarded plays no part in
solving important social questions and is believed to have no
effect on situations concerning humanity as a whole. It is considered, in short, to be of very limited importance. But if we
are to have genuine education for peace, education must be
universally considered a fundamental and indispensable
factor, the point of departure, a question of crucial interest to
all mankind.

When we consider social questions, the child is totally ignored, as if he were not a member of society at all. But if we
ponder the influence that education can have on the attainment of world peace, it becomes clear that we must make the
child and his education our primary concern. We have
realized that education can have an enormous influence on
humanity; that is why we say that education is important.

Education must no longer be regarded only as a matter of
teaching children, but as a social question of the highest importance, because it is the one question that concerns all
mankind. The many other social questions have to do with

one group or another of adults, with relatively small numbers of human beings; the social question of the child, however, has to do with all men everywhere.

Many times we find ourselves confronted with social questions that involve seemingly insoluble problems. I am convinced that our apparent inability to solve them stems from our failure to take into account one crucial factor—the human being when he is a child. We discuss many important social questions, but they all have to do with the adult; and this adult, who has thought about himself so much, who has tried to make a better life for himself, has forgotten a great part of himself, since no human being is born an adult. But at what age does a man become a man—that is, a human being, a social being, a being claiming to have certain human rights?

Man is a human being from the day he is born, even conceived.

Society until recently was concerned with children only insofar as it was necessary to provide some sort of schooling for them. Today we are concerned also about the child's physical health, but this is called hygiene, not education. We might add, moreover, that in the first years of his life, the human being is considered only from the physical point of view, as a body. At what age does he begin to be considered *human*?

It is obvious that we demonstrate a lamentable lack of conscience when we fail to recognize that the child is a personality with great human value and sacred social rights. This statement will dumbfound many people and strike them as a vast exaggeration, an absurdity. They will immediately object, "How can we be accused of lack of awareness of the child when he is the apple of our eye, our hope? How can we be accused of lack of concern when we are such conscientious parents, keenly aware of our responsibilities?" Yes, of course, we all love children, we love them a great deal, but we do not appreciate them for what they really are. We love our children or believe we love them, but we do not understand them. We do not do what we should for them, because we have no idea what it is we should do, what place they should occupy in society.

Some time ago a very important question arose—that of the role of women in society. The same kinds of things were said at that time about women as are now being said about children and their role in society.

In those days, too, it seemed absurd to speak of women as forgotten human beings. "We've neglected women, you say? How can that be, when we do everything possible for them, when we love them so much, when we protect them and are ready to die for them, when we work all our lives for them?" Nonetheless there was still such a thing as the question of woman's place in society. And there is such a thing as the question of the child's place in society.

We have been preaching for a number of years that the adult's conception of the child is mistaken. The adult commits a serious error when he takes himself for the child's creator and believes he must do everything for him. The adult regards the child more or less as an empty vessel that he must fill.

The adult believes he is the child's creator, while what he should rightly be is the servant of creation. And all he succeeds in being is a dictator, whose wishes the child must blindly obey. The adult has considered this very kind of dictatorship to be one of his own social problems, but he has never regarded it as a social problem of children.

The problem is not so easily solved as many modern pedagogues believe when they say, "Let's allow children to do whatever they like. Let's give them complete freedom and bow down to this portion of humanity." If this were done, the world would be turned upside down, and there would be a children's revolution. But what is really necessary is to realize that there is a genuine problem to be solved, a problem of education.

It is very interesting to note that the child himself is helping us solve this problem. The child obviously cannot solve it directly, but by revealing his nature to us he can help us radically change our notions of what education is and help us make our basic approach to it practical, experimental, and scientific.

As almost everyone knows, the first years of a child's life are the most important from the point of view of his physical development. We have learned that this is also true of his psychic development. If, therefore, we wish to make education a preparation for life and a means of enhancing the value of life, we must begin a child's education as soon as he is born. The most important period in education is the very first one, since at this early age the child's personality is still simple. It develops gradually, step by step. The laws of human psychic growth can then be seen quite clearly, the same way one can see through the study of embryology the development of complicated organisms that have already evolved.

What should education be like in the first years of a child's life? For us, education is not just teaching in the usual sense of passing on a body of facts to the child in school; for us, education is a form of protection, help given to obey life.

Education must help the child's psyche develop from the day he is born. The child has a psychic life from birth. A vast amount of scientific research data supporting this view is now beginning to appear. Studies of the consciousness of the newborn child and tests of infants only two hours old are among the most impressive documents of our time. From the moment he is born, the child appears as a mystery to us, a creature who might be described as a spiritual embryo.

In my book *The Secret of Childhood* I briefly discussed these important facts. The child is intelligent, and he can see and recognize things at an age when his mind was once considered to be a total blank. At the age of four months a baby has already looked at everything around him and can recognize even pictures of objects. When he is a year old he has seen so much that obvious things no longer interest him and he looks for less apparent things. When he enters his second year, he is already a snob, and it takes something more interesting, something invisible, to get him to concentrate his attention; otherwise he is quite plainly bored with everything, so much so that we were once inclined to say, "He doesn't understand yet." This is also true when he is older; school teachers know how hard it is to interest him. It is strange but true that the child might be described accurately as the most bored creature in the world. Since he is bored from the very first months of his life, he is also an unhappy creature and cries a great deal, so much that it has been said that he must cry if his voice is to develop properly. The child has a great power, a great inner sensitivity, a great drive to observe and be active. All these traits have led us to conclude that the child is a creature of intense passions. Yes, the child has a great passion to learn. If he did not, how could he find his bearings in the world? The child has natural propensities— what we might call instincts, vital drives, or inner energies— that give him a power of observation, a passion for certain things and not for others. And he has such great strength where these things are concerned that there is no other explanation for it except a kind of instinct.

I will cite an example: his sensitivity to order. Objects that are always in the same place serve as points of reference, allowing the child to orient himself as he observes his surroundings. Finding an object in a place other than its usual spot can upset a child and send him into a violent fit of tears, commonly described as a "temper tantrum." Sensitivities such as these, which often we had no idea the child possessed, and which often are very strong, help him acquire certain definite personality traits.

We call these sensitivities "sensitive periods." These sensitive periods eventually end, and if a certain trait of character is imperfectly acquired in these periods, it will always remain imperfectly developed. The developmental patterns not only of children but also of animals have been studied, and it appears that all living creatures have periods of particular sensitivity as they develop. These sensitivities disappear later, but they result in definite traits, which become permanent if they are acquired in these periods.

One of the most important things the child conquers is the use of language. A baby six months old can distinguish the sounds of the human voice from the many other noises around him, and he begins putting these sounds together. If he were a mechanism that merely heard sounds and indiscriminately mimicked them, a baby that lived next to a railroad track would whistle like a locomotive the rest of his life! But this never happens. There would seem to be something within the child that enables him to distinguish the sound of the human voice from all other sounds and makes him so fascinated by human speech that he begins to talk. There is one thing that cannot be denied—a language can be learned perfectly only in early childhood. In fact, if an adult and a young child go to live in a foreign country, the child will soon learn to speak the language of that country like a native, while the adult will always have a "foreign" accent.

The child has great powers that we adults no longer possess; he is thus a creature who is different from us. We, too, have great powers, of course. We can reason logically, for instance. But the child has a power that we do not have—that of building man himself. What is the adult to do? He is confronted with this spiritual embryo and must help him make his conquests.

If the child cannot use his intelligence it atrophies. The child needs to have something to do, to have objects on which to act. Placing such objects at his disposal means creating an environment in which he can act. When must this environment be created? As soon as the child begins to move about. Adults keep the child from being active and think that by so doing they are "training" him. The adult is a dictator. A dictator wants others to obey his will and refuses to take their personalities into account. The principal problem as the adult sees it is: How can the child be made to obey? Should he be dealt with tenderly or severely? The adult doesn't know and hence is lenient one moment and strict the next, but the child does not obey and does not mend his ways in either case. The problem therefore does not lie in how he is treated by adults. The problem is one of construction. *We must construct an environment for the child in which he can be active!*

That is why I say that an enormous problem is involved if we are to have an education capable of aiding the development of humanity. A world for children and young people must be constructed, a world of which there is no sign today.

Normality for children is closely related to their opportunities to carry on their characteristic activities. All human beings are abnormal if they cannot carry on these activities. That is why a fundamental social problem is involved.

These little human beings, who cannot speak in their own

behalf, are nonetheless saying to us, "We have a right to a world of our own." Education must begin the day the child is born, and the child must be able to live in an environment built for him, an environment that answers his needs.

A new science can thus come into being, and through it the first steps toward building a peaceful world. Harmony between the child and the adult, the creation of a place in the world for human beings who at present do not have one are goals that point to the work of reconstruction that must be undertaken.

7   The Form Education Must Take to Be Able to Help the World in Our Present Circumstances

What is the task confronting education? It is above all the task of mending breaches, filling in gaps that are vast and serious. Its primary goals must be the realization of the values of the human personality and the development of mankind.

Anyone who sets these two goals for himself might be inclined to believe that mankind's progress depends on the formation of a peace-loving human personality and that the sum total of individuals educated with such goals in mind would be a peaceful society by that very fact alone.

If we add that the effort to realize the values of man must be based on his very nature and take the natural inclinations of the child as its point of departure, people might think that it will be necessary first to determine the probable activity or future profession of the child. But I do not believe that we will attain our objective by following this path. This path would merely lead to speculation with regard to professional orientation rather than bringing about a reform of the basic organization of society. On the other hand, every time an attempt has been made to discover the true nature of the child by offering him the possibility of revealing his inner tendencies, surprising revelations have been forthcoming. The child has shown something quite unexpected, and indeed

given such striking proof of it that the facts are incontrovert-
ible. The child has said, "Don't help me. Don't bother me.
Leave me alone."

All adults have had this experience, but they have paid no
attention, or they have failed to act on the child's suggestion,
for it has seemed too simple.

When the child is given freedom to move about in a world
of objects, he is naturally inclined to perform the tasks necessary for his development entirely on his own. Let us say it
straight out—the child wants to do everything all by himself.
But the adult does not understand this, and a blind struggle
begins. The child likes neither to play idly, nor to waste time
doing useless things, nor to flit about aimlessly, as most people believe. He seeks some very precise goal, and he seeks it
with an instinctive directness of purpose. This instinct that
impels him to do things by himself makes it incumbent upon
us to prepare an environment that truly allows him to develop. When he has freed himself of the oppressive adults
who act *for* him, the child also achieves his second goal, working positively toward his own independence.

It is a commonplace that the child must be free. But what
kind of freedom has he been given? The only true freedom
for an individual is to have the opportunity to act independently. That is the condition *sine qua non* of individuality.
There is no such thing as an individual until a person can act
by himself. The instinct guiding the child to seek his independence thus leads us to realize what the whole of nature demonstrates—that any sort of association is composed
of separate individuals. Otherwise there would be no such
thing as societies, but only colonies. In the realm of nature,
we find a lower level, represented by colonies, in which individuals are only physically distinct but not autonomous, and

a higher level in which each individual is separate and independent and functions on its own. Individuality is the
basic unit, the fundamental building block of a society,
which is made up of many individuals, each functioning au-
tonomously but associating with others for a common purpose. We find many examples of this in nature. Many
members of the same species fulfill a special function together
in the maintenance of a balanced terrestrial economy. Their
action may be unlimited, whereas the function fulfilled by
colonies is always limited. The individual rarely lives a life
entirely apart from others; rather, he is meant to associate
with many others. Such an association may or may not be organized. In the latter case it does not constitute a society, but
rather an aggregate of individuals, each functioning separately.

We can thus see more clearly what these two concepts
imply. Education must foster both the development of individuality and that of society. Society cannot develop unless
the individual develops, as we learn from observing the child,
who immediately uses his newly won independence to act on
a social environment. Most of our actions would have no
reason for being if there were no other people around us, and
we do most of the things we do because we live in association
with others. As soon as the child begins to develop in an environment built for him and succeeds in acting on his own, independently of the adult, a harmony is soon established by
the child not only between himself and the environment, but
also between himself and the adult.

This process of liberation is extremely important, because
the child who is free to act becomes cured of all his psychic
deformities, or escapes them altogether, and becomes the
master of his own energies. The fact that such a transforma-

tion can come about only through free activity clearly demonstrates that a child who is deprived of such activity is a
deformed child.

It is interesting to see how character traits that are considered normal and are found in children of all races and social
backgrounds (lying, disorderliness, temper tantrums, idle
daydreaming, and so on) disappear in such an environment,
making way for totally different traits. Children's characters
change by means of a calm, constructive activity that develops
their intelligence.

Education must concern itself with the development of individuality and allow the individual child to remain independent not only in the earliest years of childhood but
through all stages of his development. Two things are necessary: the development of individuality and the participation
of the individual in a truly social life. This development and
this participation in social activities will take different forms
in the various periods of childhood. But one principle will
remain unchanged during all these stages: the child must be
furnished at all times the means necessary for him to act and
gain experience. His life as a social being will then develop
throughout his formative years, becoming more and more
complex as he grows older.

The child cannot develop if he does not have objects
around him permitting him to act. Until the present, it was
believed that the most effective learning took place when
knowledge was passed on directly to the child by his teachers.
But it is really the environment that is the best teacher. The
child needs objects to act; they are like nourishment for his
spirit.

If we think of the many things men have built in the
world, of the enormous improvement that men have brought

about in their environment, we may be led to believe that mankind's mission in the cosmos is to transform nature.

It has been said that man's greatest delight is to possess things. No! Man's greatest delight is using them! Using them to perfect himself and at the same time to improve his environment.

There is a constant interaction between the individual and his environment. The use of things shapes man, and man shapes things. This reciprocal shaping is a manifestation of man's love for his surroundings. Harmonious interaction— when it exists, as in the child—represents the normal relationship that should exist between the individual and his surroundings. And this relationship is one of love. Love impels the child not toward the possession of an object, but toward the work he can do with it. And when work begins in a certain environment, association with one's fellows also begins, for no one can work alone. And that is how life evolves: an interesting form of work appears; it enhances the value of individuality; and that in turn exalts the individual person. But if this does not happen—if something prevents the individual from acting—he begins to want to possess the things all around him. Rather than working together with others, the child quarrels with them. The result of his association with others is not collaboration but conflict.

This great revelation we owe to the child. Two paths lie open in the development of personality—one that leads to the man who loves and one that leads to the man who possesses. One leads to the man who has won his independence and works harmoniously with others, and the other to the human slave who becomes the prisoner of his possessions as he tries to free himself and who comes to hate his fellows.

These two paths might be called the paths of Good and of

Evil: one leads to Heaven and the other to Hell; one leads man to his supernatural perfection, and the other takes him below his own natural level.

Man does not take one or the other of these paths through his own free choice; the one he takes depends on whether he has developed normally or abnormally.

When individuals develop normally, they plainly feel a love not only for things, but for all living creatures. This love is not something that was taught; it is the natural result of leading the right kind of life. We might say that if love appears, we are within the range of the normal, and if it does not, within the range of the abnormal. Love is not the cause but the effect of the normal development of the individual. Certain situations in life offer the same experience. What we call love between a man and a woman, for example, is possible only when the people have reached a certain stage of development, likewise the love of a mother for her child.

Can love perhaps be taught by example? How can it be, in the absence of the cause of which this love is the effect? Can we perhaps teach brotherly love, the love of humanity, as an abstract ideal? If we are ever to realize this ideal, we will first have to organize mankind properly, in accordance with the laws of humanity. In order to be able to speak of this love, in order to be able to experience it, we must first obey the laws of human nature, or rather of human supernature. We have had many proofs that such love is possible. Many men have felt this sort of love for humanity, and it is the real essence of every individual. A few men have "rescued" themselves from the shipwreck of humanity and lived simple, active lives—the lives, in fact, of children. These men, who have won their own salvation, whom we call saints, have given the world proof of a love capable of benefiting all mankind.

The child who has felt a strong love for his surroundings

and for all living creatures, who has discovered joy and enthusiasm in work, gives us reason to hope that humanity can develop in a new direction. Our hope for peace in the future lies not in the formal knowledge the adult can pass on to the child, but in the normal development of the new man.

This is precisely what allows us to believe that a great possibility still lies before us, that there is still one hope for our salvation—a normal development that, fortunately, does not depend on what we attempt to teach the child.

What we can do is investigate this phenomenon with the objectivity of the scientist—study the facts that determine it, discover what conditions are necessary to produce it, and keep following the path that leads to normality. What we can and must do is undertake the construction of an environment that will provide the proper conditions for his normal development.

The child's psychic energy, once awakened, will develop according to its own laws and have an effect on us as well. The mere contact with a human being developing in this way can renew our own energies. The child developing harmoniously and the adult improving himself at his side make a very exciting and attractive picture.

This is the treasure we need today—helping the child become independent of us and make his way by himself and receiving in return his gifts of hope and light.

In this new picture, the adult will appear not only as the builder of the external world, but, even more importantly, as the protector of the moral and spiritual forces that appear anew in every human being born.

8   The Need for Universal Accord So That Man May Be Morally Trained to Defend Humanity

The title of this lecture points to the need to bring about a unanimous moral agreement among all men in the pursuit of one of the goals of education.

When we speak of peace, we do not mean a partial truce between separate nations, but a permament way of life for all mankind. This goal cannot be attained through the signing of treaties by individual nations. The problem for us does not lie in political action to save one nation or another; our efforts must be devoted, rather, to solving a psychological problem involving all mankind, and as a consequence acquiring a clear conception of the kind of morality necessary to defend humanity as a whole. For today it is not just one nation that is threatened with destruction, but all mankind from one end of the earth to the other, with all its various peoples at different stages of civilization.

When danger threatens a nation, all its citizens unite for its defense, and many times the very threat of danger brings unity in a country previously split into hostile political or religious factions. The danger that threatens us today has perhaps been visited upon us by destiny in order that all humanity may unite for its common defense.

If this threat has created a psychological frame of mind

70

common to everyone, it is obvious that we cannot defend ourselves against this perilous state by force of arms and that the one possible defense is a psychological one, based on a knowledge of the workings of society and on moral training.

We might well ask ourselves, "What is morality, and when does it become a weapon for the defense of mankind?"

Morality cannot be regarded in the limited sense in which we usually use the word. Our idea of morality today is expressed in a certain number of precepts—not harming others, pursuing justice, loving our fellow man as our brother. If morality is to be used as a means of defending all mankind, however, it cannot be regarded merely as a vague ideal; it must have a positive, practical basis.

First of all we must have knowledge of the human condition, of the phenomena that govern it. These phenomena are not at all evident. We seek in vain to discover in man's past any kind of lesson that will help us find our way at this juncture in our social history. There are obscure phenomena all about us, the most obscure having to do with war.

I will cite a few practical examples illustrating the extent to which we grope in the dark with regard to the causes of the psychological state that threatens to destroy humanity. Among the remedies suggested to combat the spirit of war, I have recently heard talk of the need to teach children history from a new point of view. It is evident that history as usually taught in our schools has no direct relationship to contemporary phenomena. But our analysis must not be too hasty, for if, in our attempt to remedy the situation through education, we introduce something that is useless, we will be taking the wrong road.

Wars do not occur because of rancor instilled in children through history lessons. Hatred is not what causes men to wage war today. Mankind long ago began trying to overcome what is commonly called "nationalism"—to such an extent, in fact, that until recently there were widespread complaints about the lack of patriotism.

The new view of the world set man thinking about the areas that lie beyond the boundaries of his own country, and he has continued to do so. Now men everywhere want to know what is happening in every corner of the world or to see for themselves; more and more people want to travel, to roam the earth's highways and byways; more and more people have expressed a need to learn a great many languages, or, better yet, to learn a universal language so that they can communicate more effectively with people from other countries and come into closer contact with other peoples throughout the world.

More than ever before, men are fascinated by peoples who live in distant lands: Japanese, Chinese, Indians. And more and more people are able to satisfy this great desire to see the world, for new means of transportation have permitted man to overcome formidable geographical barriers. For some time now man has clearly demonstrated his urge to mingle with other peoples, to see how others live. And the steps taken to encourage exchanges and travel abroad are a response to these new aspirations. The age-old attachment to "the place I came from" or "my part of the country" has given way to a great desire to visit every part of the globe.

We might well wonder why there has nonetheless been a concerted attempt to close down national borders, to set up customs controls and prevent currencies from being exchanged, for the sole purpose of hindering free travel from one country to another. When we ponder such absurdities, we realize that we are confronted with an enormous problem, with facts that are the prime cause of frightful depredations and yet remain mysteries to man.

Today's social organization involves mechanisms of which

the majority of mankind has no knowledge. Man is only vaguely aware that there are economic factors that determine events. But if these and other unknown factors exist, we must single them out and bring them to light.

Changing the way history is taught in schools is not so important as studying the present structure of our society—a structure of which mankind remains totally unaware, since education does not help man understand contemporary phenomena. A science that would investigate our own era, a science of peace, has become urgently necessary.

This science, in my opinion, should deal with two realities and show us how to benefit from them. The first is the fact that there is now a new kind of child; we have succeeded in furnishing the child the means necessary for his normal development, and we have thereby discovered laws that reveal man to be quite different from what he was thought in the past to be. The second is the fact that mankind today is in many respects a single nation. There are countless proofs of the unity of all mankind, from both the economic and the intellectual point of view.

The interdependence of the peoples on earth has brought about a unity among them, demonstrated by the wars of modern times. The victor today is not enriched by his victory; rather, the vanquished are a great burden upon him. This is also proved in reverse by the fact that nations that have returned to nationalism have been forced to break off many ties with other nations.

The principles of nationalism make it necessary to prevent people from leaving their own country, to put restrictions on the exchange of money, to promote in men an artificial, exaggerated attachment to their fatherlands by training them from birth to go along with what are essentially narrow national interests.

Why has such a violently coercive movement arisen in several countries? Because the ties among nations have come about only through superficial mechanisms that have had no underlying moral foundation to sustain them. Political internationalism has been based on the interests of only one sector of mankind and tends to foster a unity based on the elimination of the rights of the remainder of humanity and the destruction of their particular moral features.

It is nonetheless a proven fact that when nationalists and internationalists alike have attempted to guide a nation toward a certain goal, they have not gone about it in the same way as in the past, when attempts were made to influence the adult while the child was not considered at all. Today nationalists and internationalists alike try to indoctrinate both adults and children.

Both of these movements are powerful, and both have proponents inspired by new ideas that seem to have welled up from an abyss, like springs flowing from unfathomed depths. In nations where neither of these two currents has the upper hand, these men represent a danger that makes it imperative to take proper defensive measures.

These two movements, working at cross-purposes yet resembling each other, tend to spread like an infectious disease and make other peoples extremely fearful. The danger that these ideologies may become more and more entrenched is felt so strongly that most people resign themselves to falling under the domination of one or the other. They therefore wonder which of the two is preferable and which they should embrace. Both these movements were organized to correct social errors, and their attempts to remedy such errors have become so excessive that both are acknowledged as perilous and grievous social diseases. Choosing between the two becomes tantamount to choosing between the plague and cholera. Even if the plague could do away with cholera or vice versa, the best choice would undoubtedly be to further good health.

If humanity has reached this point today, it is a sign that our present circumstances have nothing in common with phenomena that have occurred in the past and an indication that the social structure of our time deserves study as a totally new phenomenon.

The community of interests, the unity that exists between men, stems first and foremost from scientific progress, from discoveries, inventions, and the proliferation of new machines. Through the influence of these factors, the interests of mankind have become one, but at the same time there are enormous gaps in the realm of man's psyche, and errors that set man against man have been perpetuated and remain to be corrected by education.

Contemporary man, the victim of his time, must become the master of his era. If men were prepared for their conditions of life, they would be in a position to control events rather than becoming the helpless victims of them, and they would be well on the way to social health rather than being overwhelmed by a continuous series of crises and afflictions.

Rather than being paralyzed with fear as it is today, mankind would be aware of its strength and courage and would be able to organize in order to achieve its own ends. To attain this goal, new sciences must begin, new disciplines that shed light on the new ideals and disseminate them the way conflicting ideologies have broadcast their propaganda.

I said before that the realities that can serve as a cornerstone for a new organization of mankind are twofold: the new unity of mankind and the new child.

A single nation and a better human being: these are the two great realities. The new human being must show us how to make all mankind aware of its unity. The human beings

who must bring about this new world are different from us.
Such a world is perhaps already developing without our
being aware of it. We can see the obvious portents of such a
world more or less on every hand. Amid the shadows of doubt
and fear that hang heavily over the human race, we can now
catch a glimpse of the light that will dissipate them, because a
new society is already coming into being. A new humanity
for a new world is already being born!

9   Fifth Lecture

The education that will lead the way to a new humanity has one end alone: leading the individual and society to a higher stage of development. This concept involves many factors and may seem obscure, but it becomes clearer if we realize that mankind has to fulfill a collective mission on earth, a mission involving all of humanity and therefore each and every human being. This concept may enable us to set a definite goal for our efforts. But what can this mission of humanity be?

Is this mission the predominance of one nation over another? The power of the people? Industrial or cultural progress? And what will the individual regard as his personal mission? Ensuring that he and others have the means to survive? Ensuring the possibility of securing an education? It would seem that above and beyond these goals, which have to do with the interests of specific individuals or groups, there is something that involves all mankind and perhaps even the universe itself, creation, cosmic harmony.

This "something" might be considered as involving a religious ideal. But what I should like to discuss is the possibility that science may have a predominant role to play in helping us discover this single universal mission.

It is possible to consider the life of the creatures of the

earth from a single point of view, and I would like to make a few remarks about the modern study of geology and evolution.

The most interesting, and indeed almost awesome, fact resulting from such study is that the earth is a creation of life. Life created rocks and soil, and it is life that sustains the harmony of the earth. Yes, the earth is the handiwork of living things. The oceans are kept in constant chemical balance by living things, and living things also maintain the purity of the air.

All creatures who live on earth have a cosmic role to play. The maintenance of life on earth depends on many species, each one of which has a special, specific function. Animals feed and live and reproduce; each one has a life cycle that fulfills a special role in relation to the life of other species. Everyone knows, for instance, that the disappearance of one species in a certain place upsets the balance, because the lives of all species are interrelated. Life therefore can be regarded as an energy that maintains life itself.

I would now like to pose a question: does not man also have a cosmic mission to fulfill on earth? Is it conceivable that this being who has such great intelligence, who is the worker par excellence, has no part to play in the labor of the cosmos?

Human energy, too, has appeared on earth to undertake and fulfill a specific mission.

It is quite evident that man has a mission. He has extracted hidden wealth and marvelous energies from the bowels of the earth, and he has created a superworld, or, more precisely, a supernature. As he has constructed this supernature little by little, man has also perfected himself and made the natural man he was into a supernatural man. Nature is a domain that has existed for centuries, and supernature is yet another domain, which man has gradually constructed.

Contemporary man no longer lives within nature, but within supernature. An animal can procure its food directly from the earth, but man is dependent on other men. How many men labor so that the bread we eat may reach our mouths! And fruit that comes to us from a faraway place may represent a vast organization of men, a formidable and strict organization, that holds human society together.

We must be aware of this organization if we are to evaluate properly certain widespread ideas that find expression in a number of slogans: "Let us return to nature." "Let us become one with nature."

The life that some call "artificial" is mankind's supernatural life. Our way of life is not artificial, but rather the product of labor. If we did not make such a distinction, we might be inclined to say that even the way of life of certain animals is artificial—that of bees, who "artificially" produce honey, for instance. Man is a great worker, capable of creating a supernature through his labors.

But we might now ask ourselves: if animals labor so joyously, why do men not also take delight in their work? Man should be much happier than animals. His unhappiness is proof that there must be errors inherent in human society and in the supernature that humanity has constructed. Man must labor not only to support himself and his family, but also to become an instrument of something great and awesome—not only to serve his individual interests, but also to serve humanity as a whole. From this point of view, the history of humanity becomes very interesting. As we study man from this perspective, we witness first his effort to explore the earth and extract its riches and then his effort to explore the heavens and master the energies of the intangible, the infinite, the limitless. An enormous, immense human conquest! And yet man today considers mere physical survival a problem.

Man is not conscious of his mission, nor of the heights that he has reached. Humanity has fallen sick, like an organism suffering from a circulatory disease; man is weak and unhappy. Yet he continues to pursue his irresistible mission, and humanity is now united as one single nation.

And man, that feeble and unhappy creature, may be cured if he so wills. He need only open his eyes, rectify his errors, and realize his powers. When we say that man must intensify the means of communication and interchange available to him, we are pointing to a goal that he cannot attain immediately. Humanity must first be convinced of the urgency of attaining this goal. Man must be educated. It is true that education can create a better kind of man, but this is a vast undertaking. It is a labor that may well take a long time, but it will nonetheless be brief in comparison with the work that man has already accomplished.

The first thing that must be done is to construct an environment that answers the needs of young people. What has been done to date with regard to that period of human life that precedes maturity? What has been done for children, for young people? Practically nothing, or at any rate very little. Unlike animals, who build extensively for their young, man, the intelligent being who labors with his own hands, has failed to build on a similar scale for his progeny. What has the world, with its wealth of great constructions, with all its comforts, done on behalf of children? It is not enough to love in an abstract way; we must begin to do something concrete, something practical—to construct the supernature necessary for the life of children and young people.

I would like to review briefly what we have done along these lines.

We have constructed, first of all, an environment providing all the little things necessary for the life of children. The child has not said thank you, but he has revealed to us the hidden treasure of man's soul. And this knowledge of the human soul, of its grandeur and power, represents both a warning and a hope for us.

Let us therefore continue our efforts! Let us construct an environment for children and young people; the thanks we will receive for so doing will be the enlightenment we need to see all the errors inherent in the supernature that we adults have created only for ourselves. We must build something new, not offer older children the same things we offer the young ones. Miniature objects and utensils no longer satisfy seven-year-old children. They need other things. The four walls of a "house"[1] become too confining; older children need to go out and explore the world. They must have broader social horizons. Man feels a great need to make genuine efforts, so as to measure his own worth; the Boy Scout movement has partially answered this need. The idea of organizing young people is not an error. The mistake arises when the most intimate needs of the individual young person are not satisfied.

It is time now to correct these errors, to bring about a great reform, to offer young people the means necessary for their development and the enhancement of their personalities.

This task cannot be entrusted to private efforts alone; it is society as a whole that is called upon to fulfill it. It is of vital interest to the state to organize the life of young people. The

[1]The Montessori environment for children between two and one-half and six years of age is called "House of the Children."

child by the age of twelve should already be taking an active part in social life; he should be producing, selling, and working, not in order to learn a trade, but because working means coming into contact with life, participating in the building of supernature. These young people should engage in economic transactions, learn the value of money, and take conscious part in productive activities.

Objects made carefully by hand have today been replaced by articles mass-produced by machines, a change made necessary by the fact that men's lives proceed at a more and more frantic pace. But handicrafts, which produce beautiful objects, and which society is now attempting to revive, could well be entrusted to young people. Let us hope that the art of fine craftsmanship is not lost simply because machines exist. May young people be given the possibility of continuing to lovingly produce beautiful things! And the creative spirit of young people can accomplish many other things as well. Botany, for instance, requires a keen eye and accurate judgment. Young people can become passionately involved in doing calm, serene, beautiful work that enables their young personalities to develop and find worthwhile goals. If young people at a certain point are called upon to take an active part in the life of humanity, they must first feel that they have a great mission to accomplish and prepare themselves for it. They must have the chance to meditate upon it a little. We call this period "the period of the desert." Christ himself as he emerged from childhood went off into the desert before beginning his great mission. The man prepared in this way will fulfill his mission faithfully and consciously.

The young person today is urged to study, to buckle down, to conserve his time, to get ahead in the world. Poor thing. When he has completed his studies, he knows nothing of social life, and he feels lost and forsaken. Why should he have worked so hard? Why should he have studied, if books are no longer of any importance?

I cannot discuss the subject at greater length. I will simply say that as we see it, man must be inspired to seek universality until the day he dies. Man thus prepared, conscious of his mission in the cosmos, will be capable of building the new world of peace.

10 Lecture Closing the Congress

In behalf of all the members of the congress, I should like to extend my warm thanks to the city of Copenhagen for having offered us such generous hospitality and to the officials of the Danish government who have kindly taken part in our congress, thus supporting the great social question of our time—the social question of the child.

I should also like to thank the governments of those nations that sent delegates to the congress to demonstrate their moral support for the sacred cause of the child.

I should like to thank, finally, all those members of the congress who came from distant countries, who attend our meetings each year and thus faithfully prove by their example the determination of all of us to remain united in this effort to redeem mankind. They have come here from many faraway countries, including even America, and their presence, I repeat, demonstrates the importance today of releasing human moral values from the threatening shadows that surround them.

The theme of our congress has been Educate for Peace. Those who have taken part have come because of their interest in education, of course, but they have also been attracted by the goal we have set for education—the attainment of peace. By coming, they have given proof of their good will, and in view of the goal that we have set ourselves, we hope that they will be prepared not only to embrace the ideas proposed, but also to take concrete steps to carry them out, for peace can be brought about only through positive action.

So how can we, then, unite our efforts and work together to achieve concrete ends?

The first and most important step is for each of us to examine his own conscience, realize his own shortcomings and defects, and seek to remedy them.

Would putting an end to injustices be a step toward peace? If so, we must begin by recognizing the greatest injustice of all—our injustice toward the child, which is not limited to any one group or nation, but is universal.

Or is social progress perhaps the road to peace? In that case, we must not forget that there is one vast sector of humanity that we must still make a radical effort to set free children.

Do we believe and constantly insist that cooperation among the peoples of the world is necessary in order to bring about peace? If so, what is needed first of all is collaboration with children. Adults have worked hard in their own behalf. They have already achieved much while trying to put an end to injustice, and they have actively sought cooperation, but to no avail, because something fundamental is missing. It is fruitless to expend a great deal of effort when there is no foundation on which to build.

All our efforts will come to nothing until we remedy the great injustice done the child, and remedy it by cooperating with him. If we are among the men of good will who yearn for peace, we must lay the foundation for peace ourselves, by working for the social world of the child.

The figure of the child must be a shining symbol beckoning us on, a symbol pointing not only to the goal to be attained, but also to the one path that will enable us to reach it.

The child is usually regarded as a tiny creature who needs help, who must be aided when he is in pain, who must be comforted when he cries, who must be healed when he is sick. But it was Christ who showed us what the child really is, seeing in him something new and surprising—the adult's guide to the Kingdom of Heaven, the model the adult must imitate in order to change himself.

This conception is perhaps still too lofty, too far removed from the practical considerations that have continued to limit our view of what a child really is. Concrete psychological proof of his true nature must be given. And precisely because there is now definite experimental evidence proving it, we have taken upon ourselves to proclaim this conception of the child. Our experiences with children have revealed things of which we were once totally unaware, things that must be taken into account if we are to proceed along the road to peace.

But even if we do not care to take this spiritual dimension into account and merely limit ourselves to practical considerations, we are still obliged to view him in a new light.

We want the child to be recognized, socially speaking, as a citizen, as a dignified human being with a right to live and be protected. Whatever his social background, whatever his racial origins, whatever his birthplace, the child must be recognized as a citizen.

Let us look for a moment at the recent social advances man has made. Human beings have acquired many rights and have won freedom in many areas—slaves, women, and workers have been freed. But these solutions have affected only adults directly. Though many advances have been made and many new laws passed, the child still remains a forgotten citizen, and nothing has been done for him. Childhood has remained little more than a stage to pass through on the way to adulthood, and the child has not been recognized as an independent person with rights of his own.

The French Revolution brought a Declaration of the Rights of Man. Among them was the right to an education. But what has become of this right? All that it has meant is that the child has been burdened with all the labor needed to provide the adult with culture. His sufferings, his desires have not counted; the one thing that has mattered was to secure for the adult the enjoyment of a right he claimed for himself.

It would take far too much time for me to paint the whole picture of our tragic lack of understanding of children. The world today, however, is beginning to realize that the life of the child is fraught with repression and injustices that must be remedied.

The principal message we have sought to preach is the need to construct an environment. This is not a materialistic notion; it has a solid foundation in man's soul, for it takes into account something hidden deep within it. This social environment for the child must serve to protect him not in his weakness but in his inherent grandeur, for he possesses enormous potential energies that promise to benefit all mankind.

This task of protecting him, which is also a task of educating and reeducating adults, is an effort to guard the greatest treasure we possess, one that can guide us toward that light that we sum up in a single word: peace.

Discussion or meditation on the sufferings of the child will not help us; what we need is a new approach involving a new way of thought. The path then becomes clear and easy to follow. And just as there is not a single man or woman anywhere who has not been a child and who will not readily admit that every capacity he or she possesses was acquired in childhood, so society must be led to see that this is true of its powers as well. The future action of humanity cannot be unilateral. Nothing can be achieved in the world of the adult that is not first achieved in the world of the child. We must therefore follow a twofold path and consider two parts in humanity—that which is forming itself and that which applies its formation. Every act that the adult performs in the social order must also be performed in the social life of children. Every law for adults must be accompanied by a corresponding law for children; every new discovery that furthers the life of the adult must also be devoted to the life of the child—not only houses for adults, but also houses for children; not only objects for adults, but also objects for children; not only rights for adults, but also rights for children. I also believe that the child should have representatives in the legislative bodies of his country. Those assemblies in which the laws are discussed and the material and intellectual interests of mankind are considered should have representatives to defend the interests of this very large part of humanity: children. There should likewise be a ministry for childhood, as for every other area of great general interest. There should be a minister for the protection of humanity— that is, a minister for children.

A minister of education is not enough. Such a minister is concerned only with one particular problem; he is interested in the child only when he has reached a certain point of development and is old enough to attend school. The social question of the child should be considered from both legal and practical points of view, and we should be concerned with him from the day he is born, even conceived. As this congress closes, I would like to plant the first seeds of a social movement on behalf of the child by doing something practical and concrete: founding the *Party of the Child*.

We call upon everyone, those who are present and those who are not, and invite them to participate in this work for the defense of the human race and civilization. Viewed in this light, the protection of the child is a great new undertaking that by releasing the values of one part of humanity will enable all of us to bring about a better world. This is the path that leads to peace.

The primary goal of this social party of the child is to bring about a recognition of the dignity of children and young people and to secure for them the place in society that they should rightfully have in these enlightened times. To achieve this goal we wish to appeal not only to educators, but also to the general public, and especially to those who are aware of their duties as parents; for it is up to parents to defend the rights of their children. The child in fact is not helplessly cast out onto the face of the earth by nature; he is entrusted to the care of a father and a mother whose mission it is to love and cherish him. This union between parents and children can lead us further along the road to civilization where both generations are given new social responsibilities. For all humans of every race and every country on earth have children, and the child can become the focus of universal interests and ends. The aim of the social party of the child is thus not only to protect society from many current evils, but to create a sphere of action that will enable all mankind to work together.

11 My Method

When I see before me such a large and distinguised audience, I am deeply moved, for I know that those who have come to hear me speak have done so not out of personal loyalty to me but because it has been announced that my subject will be children. This fact touches me deeply because it leads me to believe that the world is reawakening and wants to learn about this new king that has been born—the child.

This evening's subject, My Method, is one that I feel very uncomfortable discussing. I might even say, though my listeners may not believe me, that I find this the most difficult subject of any on which to deliver a public lecture, for I have not evolved a method of education. As a matter of fact, when one attempts to explain this method in concrete terms, it is necessary to discuss child psychology, for it is the psychology of the child, the life of his soul, that has gradually dictated what might be called a pedagogy and a method of education. If I can be said to have a method of education, it is one based on the psychic development of the normal child.

All other methods of education have taken the work of certain adults as their point of departure and have sought to educate or teach the child according to programs dictated by adults. For my part, I believe that the child himself must be

the pivot of his own education—not the child as people ordinarily think of him, but rather his innermost soul, seen from
a perspective that was unprecedented before the advent of
what has been called the Montessori Method.

A little parable may help illustrate the idea I am trying to
express. Suppose that we have a diamond imbedded in a dull
matrix and that we remove the surrounding material to
reveal the bright jewel. Seeing the jewel, some might ask,
"How have you gone about obtaining a precious stone that
reflects the light so perfectly?" We would reply that we are
not the creators of this marvelous jewel; it already existed,
buried deep within the extraneous matter surrounding it.
The same can be said of the child. He has shown us how he
should be treated and has revealed his splendor to us.

In going about his dedicated labors in behalf of the child,
the adult must realize above all else that his task concerns a
revelation of the child's soul. If he does so, the steps he
subsequently takes and the aid he offers the child will be of
great importance; if he does not do so, all his work will go for
nothing. This work must have a twofold objective: constructing a suitable environment and bringing about a new
attitude toward children on the part of adults.

Two factors must be present if the child is to develop. It is
necessary to create surroundings for the child that answer his
needs not only from the point of view of his physical health
but also from the point of view of his spiritual life.

The child must be able to act freely in such an environment. There he must find motives for constructive activity
that corresponds to his developmental needs. He must have
contact with an adult who is familiar with the laws governing
his life and who does not get in his way by overprotecting
him, by dictating his activities, or by forcing him to act
without taking his needs into account.

In such an environment, the child proves to be something quite different from a creature who enjoys wasting time and wants to do nothing but play. He becomes an individual who works very hard, who is very observant, who is not destructive. He is incredibly meticulous (much more so than we adults are); he performs tasks scrupulously; he is capable of great concentration; he is able to control the movements of his body; and he is a great lover of silence. He is punctual in obedience; he obeys promptly, and he delights in obeying. He works very well by himself and feels no need to compete with other children. All this is the result of an interchange between the child and his surroundings, between the child and his work. It does not come about because there is an adult who guides every step, an adult who lords it over the child. On the contrary, the adult who comes into intimate contact with such children is well aware that new and mysterious feelings are awakened in him, and he begins to step aside. He acquires a sort of humility, for he thinks, "This child can do so many things without my direct help, without my urging him to do them."

The child thus is possessed of marvelous directives that come to him from within and from this social environment created for him. This has been proved over and over again. Thirty or forty children work together in beautiful, attractive surroundings created especially for them. If the teacher must leave the room, the children continue working. Their normal activities go on as before, and all of them pursue their work by themselves. And we often hear such snatches of conversation as:

"Who taught you that?"

"I learned it by myself."

"Which of you did that?"

"I though *I* should do it."

This development takes place because the child has been able to work and to be in direct contact with reality. It does not come from anything we teach the child; it is a definite, constructive process, a natural phenomenon that results when the child is given the chance to make his own efforts and do his own work without intermediaries.

We think the child is happiest when he is playing; but the truth is that the child is happiest when he is working.

For the benefit of those who know nothing about our method, I shall describe what we have done for little children. When they have reached the age of about three, we provide them with an environment containing useful household articles: child-size brooms, crockery, tables, and so on. The greatest delight of these children is doing tasks perfectly, and they busy themselves doing something all the time. What is more, these children's attitudes at home also change a great deal, and their families come and ask us, "Explain to us why it is that our children are so well behaved now and such hard workers!" It seems strange, but often such illnesses as anemia, digestive disturbances, and so on disappear, proving that children in ordinary surroundings suffer when they have no outlet for their inner need to develop by being active. The children in the first schools we set up were from very poor families. The first group we worked with was made up of children of day laborers, who had to go and seek work and simply left their children by themselves on the streets. The children were timid and had all the other personality traits of abandoned children. But even though they had suffered great psychological traumas, these children gradually became happy, serene little creatures in the special environment created for them. What is more, children from wealthy families, who always have many people around them, who never know a moment's freedom, and who are usually the most

difficult to discipline in traditional schools, gradually came to
be like the others, too.

The characters of all children change in this environment
where they can work without being disturbed, and they
become calm and able to concentrate.

I would not like to lead you to believe that this kind of environment works miracles all by itself and that the adult has
no part to play in it. The adult does have a role to play. He
must show the child how to use objects correctly; he must
show him, for example, how to polish metal. And in order to
do this, he must get all the necessary things ready—bits of
rag, metal polish, and so on—and he should be quite
"finicky," so to speak, about the whole procedure, because it
is this very meticulousness that arouses the child's interest.
The child watches the adult working methodically and
carefully and repeats his actions methodically and carefully.
But once he has put a perfect polish on the metal object and
not a speck of tarnish remains, he does an amazing thing,
which we adults would surely not do—he goes on polishing it
and often begins all over again a second, third, and even
fourth time.

What motivates the child is thus not the goal set for him by
the adult, but his own drive for self-perfection. The child
perfects himself through contact with reality, through activity that absorbs all his attention.

The child has his own way of working, a way different
from ours that we must understand and respect. To our adult
way of thinking, the child should polish the metal object only
once, and we might be tempted to prevent him from doing it
over again; but this repetition permits an inner development
that will manifest itself later in surprising ways.

The child can repeat a particular activity a great many
times. An experiment in psychology demonstrated this when

children were given certain tasks to perform. A three-year-old child given a cylinder block fitted the ten cylinders into their holes more than forty times and was so oblivious to his surroundings as he did so that he did not even notice external stimuli. This concentration is undoubtedly a means of development.

The child must always be given work to do with his hands as he works with his mind, for the child's personality has a functional unity. In traditional classrooms, however, the child is not given tasks calling for simultaneous motor activity and mental effort. Our principle of functional unity has enabled us to fulfill an extremely important goal of education —offering the child the possibility of coming into direct contact with reality. The fact that a three-year-old child is able to concentrate on objects for long periods of time has proved to us that the child has much greater powers than was commonly believed. In traditional schools children are assigned tasks that do not interest them because they are too easy. We must investigate and discover the limits of the difficulties the child can handle and discover the level that keeps him most interested.

We have learned another intriguing fact. Children find it very hard to concentrate on spoken words, but they have no difficulty concentrating on objects. This immediately suggests the reason for two great difficulties the teacher in the traditional classroom faces. The first is the difficulty of imparting knowledge orally, which is generally recognized; the second is the difficulty of keeping the child's attention. The problem of teaching children cannot be solved by having good textbooks or by getting a good teacher into the classroom to say the right things about objects that the child cannot see, but rather by building a life-environment that contains objects that will concretely represent the things to be learned. This problem is now being studied intensively, and newer teaching methods utilize physical objects more and more extensively as educational tools. It still is not widely recognized, however, that all schoolchildren in the traditional classroom are painfully bored, because their teachers set them tasks that are too easy and therefore fail to hold their interest.

The human being needs to know things, and he is much more capable of learning spontaneously than we have supposed. It is also true, however, that if a child's intelligence is not stimulated he withdraws and his interest flags. The majority of children are thus condemned to waste their childhood and never realize their potential.

There is another very important factor determining a child's interest. Children's interests do not remain the same as they pass through the various stages of childhood. Moreover, children do not have a linear pattern of development. What interests a child today will not interest him at all when he is older. If we attempt to teach the same thing to a child of five and one of eight, the latter will not learn so quickly. This is so, I repeat, because what arouses a child's interest at one age will fail to do so at another age.

One of the problems of teaching is thus to discover the subjects best suited to children of different ages—or rather, those best suited to their different interests. Our experience has demonstrated, for instance, that children are much more interested in learning the alphabet at age four than at any other age. Children at this age delight so much in writing that we have called this phenomenon the "explosion into writing," but if they are taught to write as late as the age of six this "explosion" does not take place. The troubles that children ordinarily encounter learning mathematics or grammar are easily overcome if difficult problems in these areas are presented at exactly the right moment. In my two recent books, *Psychoarithmetic* and *Psychogeometry*, I describe experiences with seven-year-old children. They were able to do advanced arithmetic and algebra exercises that usually are not assigned to children until high school, since mathematics and geometry do in fact present genuine difficulties when they are taught orally. But these difficulties are easily overcome if we use material that concretely illustrates mathematical abstractions. Such material enables the child to learn according to the laws of mental development. As we have observed children, we have seen that they practice a great deal in order to learn something. They will repeat an exercise a hundred and even two hundred times without becoming bored. As a matter of fact, they find such repetition restful and reassuring. It is clear that the psychic process of learning that takes place within the child is of such a nature that it is impossible for us to view his mind merely as a mirror that passively reflects images.

Learning means working long and hard. There are children who go through long arithmetical operations because they find them really fascinating. I once saw a child multiply a thirty-two-figure number by a twenty-figure number. Such operations are so tiresomely complicated that we adults would find them tedious, but the child does them for the sake of doing them, spontaneously. Both the younger and the older child feel a need to do exercises over and over, and to follow their own path of development by their own means.

From another point of view, school would seem to be the place where man develops through acquiring culture. But culture is a *means*, not an end. Properly understood, this fact makes the work of teachers, professors, and parents much easier and completely changes our ideas about education.

Doubtless the fact that the child learns by himself, that he can overcome so many difficulties by himself, gives him an inner satisfaction that enhances his sense of personal dignity. The possibility of choosing his own activities also helps foster traits that we do not ordinarily think of as characteristic of the child—a sense of independence and a sense of initiative, for example.

Culture cannot be all of man's life. Man is not just a creature with an intellect, and instruction cannot satisfy all his needs. I believe that we must do much more to educate children and young people. Just as we have built an environment that answers the needs of small children, so we must prepare an environment in the outside world that will foster social education for older children. The traditional classroom is no longer enough. A child may learn much more than his fellows there and still know nothing about the world and have no real character.

Raising the level of mankind cannot be achieved through culture alone. The problem is much more complex, and it is imperative that we solve it as rapidly as possible. We need to construct a social environment, a new world for the child and the adolescent, so that their individual consciences may develop. A vast educational reform and above all a vast social reform are called for today.

III
The Importance of Education in Bringing About Peace

12   First Lecture

Professor Jordan has asked me not to deliver a series of lectures as if this were a classroom, but to take the opportunity of being here to establish a contact of the spirit with you and to tell you what feelings I have when I work with children.

When I am in the midst of children I do not think of myself as a scientist, a theoretician. When I am with children I am a nobody, and the greatest privilege I have when I approach them is being able to forget that I even exist, for this has enabled me to see things that one would miss if one were somebody—little things, simple but very precious truths. It is not always imperative to see big things, but it is of paramount importance to see the beginnings of things. At their origins there are little glimmers that can be recognized as soon as something new is developing. They become a bright light that will bring us a much better understanding of the complicated labyrinth that the social life of the adult represents.

The child is a spiritual embryo that develops spontaneously, and if we follow him from the beginning, he can reveal many things to us. Social life today is extremely complex,

The following series of addresses was given at the International School of Philosophy in Amersfoort on December 28, 1937.

fraught with errors and incomprehensible contradictions. These are days of gloom, a time of spiritual darkness. The prophecy of the Bible, "A day will come when we shall be swallowed up in darkness," has come true. The phenomena around us remain impenetrable. We no longer understand the origins of the things in the outside world that men themselves have constructed or are constructing. We find ourselves today in a world that is a marvel, thanks to the discoveries of science. But while we can bask in the light of these outer achievements, we are enveloped in darkness spiritually.

Though man now has powers over and beyond nature, though he can span enormous distances, though he is the master of the energies of the universe, he is a bewildered and panic-stricken creature. Contemporary man is like a child lost in the forest. He is not afraid of the things he can see nor of animals that may be lurking about, but of little things, of the rustle of leaves and the echo of ghostly footsteps. He is terrified of things that do not really exist.

Man needs spiritual tranquillity and peace; he needs light. Who can offer him a little light?

Even reading the most current books will not enlighten us. In his search for the causes of the phenomena about him, man has obviously learned an enormous number of things about his environment. He has mastered all the secrets of nature and all its energies. But there is still one thing that remains unknown to him, and that unknown is man himself.

It would be an exhausting task to list all man's discoveries in the physical world. But what discoveries has man made about himself, about his life, his ends, or truth and error?

Man has simply followed his intuition over and over again. The world has changed, but what has changed in man? Which of his feelings? Which of his prejudices?

Man remains a mystery, as expressed in the title of the

book *Man the Unknown*. Man's soul is an enigma. It has remained an unknown that inhabits an unknown domain. Not even psychology has been able to enlighten us, to shed light on the mystery.

Psychology has considered only discrete phenomena in the human subconscious and has not seen the essence, the truth. The interpretation of discrete phenomena cannot decipher the riddle of man the unknown. But is man doomed by his very nature to remain absolutely unknown?

I say no, not necessarily. But I must add that man, if repressed, might remain an unknown to himself forever. We are not the ones who can show man what he is.

One truth must be repeated again and again. The child alone can reveal to us the secrets of the spiritual life of man. And in order for this revelation to be received, it is necessary for adults to cease to exist, to empty themselves completely so that the child may enter the void and fill it.

The child—the spiritual embryo—reveals himself to us adults in order to guide us through the labyrinth. The child brings us light amid the shadows that surround us.

Something similar has happened in biology. How can an organism be understood if it is studied only after it has fully developed? It was only when biologists began studying organisms in the process of development, when the invention of the microscope made it possible to observe cell division, that we really understood them. Embryology shed light on all of biology.

Simplicity reveals important truths to us; usually the secret of the truth lies in simple things.

It is difficult to understand a complicated society, organized by oppressed men whose natures are distorted from the moment they are born, whose lives are condemned at their very roots. What has the child taught us? When a child lives in an atmosphere congenial to his vital needs, he proves to have character traits quite different from those we usually consider him as having. He provides living proof that mankind can change and improve from its very origin. But the world of adults must change. We must unite; we must reach out to the child, have faith in him, construct the proper climate for him and change our very selves.

The child then promises the redemption of humanity, and we might say that this truth is represented by the mystical symbol of the Nativity. The child must no longer be considered as the son of man, but rather as the creator and the father of man, pointing the way to a better life and bringing us light. The child should be regarded as the father of the man, the father capable of creating a better humanity. It is incumbent upon us, therefore, to serve the child and create an atmosphere that can satisfy his needs.

If we provide such an environment, we are able to see how he develops. I would like to mention a few points that directly concern our own life. The child has proved to have instincts whose existence we did not even suspect. He has proved to possess a surprising fundamental instinct—he wants to *work*. We do not use the term *work* in the ordinary sense of the word. The child teaches us that work is not a virtue, not an effort that man is forced to make; it is not the need to earn a livelihood. *Work is man's fundamental instinct.*

Man can be cured of his psychic ills by working; he can break through to a genuinely spiritual life by working. Work is the means of remedying all his shortcomings; a number of traits that we observe in children are not at all typical of the ordinary adult. Man is born to work. The instinct to work is his most outstanding trait. We must change our lives, for much that we ordinarily consider good or bad in our lives is not really so at all.

We regard it as good if a child shows affection; obedience is taken to be the moral virtue par excellence; being able to sit quietly and being imaginative are considered good. But all these traits disappear as the child works. Flightiness, laziness, rebelliousness, and deceitfulness disappear also. What is left then?

What is left is the *new man*, who has none of our defects— the man who works diligently, the man who is healed of all his ills.

This man has genuine qualities—love, which is something different from attachment; discipline, which is something different from blind submission; the ability to relate to reality, which is something different from flights of fancy. The child brings us light; he shows us the new man, the moral man, and teaches us the value of simple and regular habits, for simplicity and regularity are the keys to well-being.

I have mentioned love. The child has taught us fundamental things about love. When we observe animal life in a natural environment, we see evidence of maternal love and family love. We are aware of certain forms of love, but others remain completely unknown to us unless someone demonstrates them.

The child has given us striking revelations of different kinds of love, all of them directly related to work. Most of us experience the kind of love that causes us to be deeply attached to others; but this is a passing love. There is ample reason, however, to believe that the human spirit is inherently capable of another kind of love that is not transitory, that does not change, that does not die. Man expresses this by saying that he loves something that transcends his family—he speaks of his love of his country, of his love of God.

Man has had intimations of this higher form of love because he has intuitions within his soul of every truth, though he has not often followed and applied them in his everyday life. This higher love comes naturally to children, however, and is characteristic of them.

This love is the essential fire in man, without which he cannot live. It is not simply tender affection. I assure you that I have seen this love; I have been amazed by it; I have called it "love for one's environment." What do I mean by this? What is this love like?

The child supposedly likes bright colors and pretty things. When he sees bright colors and pretty things, he experiences a certain sensation, but he does not feel love. What he feels is a sensory phenomenon, which is accompanied by a desire to possess, for sensations involve not only a neural reaction but a psychic reaction as well.

Usually when we see something we feel a desire to possess it. The more a person possesses, the more he wants to possess. All men, rich and poor alike, want to possess things. And we really should think of them not as normal men, but as sick men.

There are social movements that aim to strip others of their possessions. Society has organized certain channels for man's urge to possess. In the deviated human adult we see a tendency to possess and a drive for power that are entirely different from those of the normal man. In the abnormal child we see clear evidence of this urge to possess. The child never stops asking for things, and the more he is given, the more he wants to have. He is a child who does not work, who has sensations but does not love.

The love of one's environment is the secret of all man's progress and the secret of social evolution. It becomes manifest in people who have survived life's vicissitudes, who have been able to keep their integrity, or who have rediscovered such integrity within themselves. Love of the environment inspires man to learn, to study, to work. What is the

difference then between the sort of love that leads to possession and the sort of love that leads to knowledge?

Love spurs man to learn. It leads to intimate contact between the thing that is loved and the human spirit, which in
turn leads to production. Labor, life, and normal human development result. Love leads human beings to study things
that seem repellent to most of us. In the United States there
was a man who had a love of this kind for snakes, and he
devoted his life to studying their habits. The object of such a
love is not important. What is important is that love spurs
man to use his mind, to produce, to labor. All the products of
civilization are the result of man's labor. Every new thing
that comes into being is produced by men who love their environment: bread, dwelling places, furniture, and so on. Everything in our social environment is the result of some form
of labor.

Men who have come to experience love are privileged.
When there is an interchange between an object and a man's
spirit, something deep inside him is awakened—human dignity.

Love is the instinct that guides our actions. Even animals
have such an instinct. If it is not aroused in man, he will not
have a normal life. Instead of finding his work absorbing, it
will exhaust him and he will feel hatred rather than love. Fatigue and hatred are dark shadows of the urge to possess that
cloud men's minds. Man's errors stem from hatred.

People try to teach children nice manners. But children
who are allowed to develop normally are loving creatures
who are naturally kind and polite to one another. The traditional rules of good breeding become superfluous if a refined
spiritual sensitivity reigns. If it is absent, however, "proper"
behavior must be learned by the book. Outward rules of behavior are necessary only when man is insensitive and un-
feeling. Everything must then be taught; everything becomes

a burden to us. We are slaves; we must be trained to love one another, and it becomes a great effort. Loving one another is impossible in an atmosphere of hatred.

Our will to power and possession enslaves us, and instead of a human society based on love and justice we have a society in which all men must hide behind masks in order to live. Work, which should be a source of joy, becomes a burden. Let us remember the curse visited upon Adam, "In the sweat of thy face shalt thou eat bread."

If the adult did not take the wrong path—as a result of his having been a neglected, mistreated child—he would feel a love for his environment and a love of work. He would be a normal man. Love is a goal to be attained, not a starting point. Sermons on love will not help us; it is not by force of will that we can produce love. Its basis is moral health. There have been exceptional human beings who have proved that such love is possible—Saint Francis of Assisi, for one.

Now that we have caught a glimpse of what a normal man can be, we have reason to believe that all mankind may one day become better, become normal.

Man experiences a spiritual sensation that uplifts him, that gives him intimations of glory—his love for his environment. This divine awakening spurs him on toward a mystical goal —the creation of a supernature.

Man must conquer the earth. If he has not developed normally, he must do so by means of violence and hatred. If he has developed into a truly normal man, he will find the happiness of healthy life in his effort. Man must obey the laws that rule his life and, because they are hidden, he must look for them.

13   Supernature and the Single Nation

The study of nature and the observation of animal development have provided a comprehensive framework for the explanation of certain social phenomena.

Darwin's theory, as set forth in his writings on the struggle for survival, natural selection, and the survival of the fittest, has helped us understand the major events in world history. In his various works he advanced the idea that man is a privileged species, outlined the nature of human conflicts, and showed us the fate of those who proved weak in the struggle for survival.

There are other essential phenomena in human life, of course. Some of them, in particular those having to do with infancy and the helplessness of creatures who are not yet able to fight for their survival, cannot be explained or solved by Darwin's theory. Another factor that Darwinian theory fails to explain adequately is the protection that the adult offers the newborn being as he first confronts life in order that he may acquire the chief characteristics of the species as a whole.

Do we not find something similar in the life of animal species? When mature animals reach the point in their life cycle at which they must protect their young, a radical transformation occurs with regard to their aggressive instincts. Their relationships with other animals change completely;

they no longer fight one another, and even very fierce animals become gentle.

Important changes also can be observed in insects. In an effort to prepare a protective environment for their young, they begin—even before the young ones are born—to carry out real work and to build shelters. The protective instinct guides their labor.

The curious thing is that human beings, the builders par excellence, have not demonstrated a similar strong and conscious instinct to protect their young. If we compare humans with bees, we see that these insects selflessly work to serve their species, whereas humans do not bother to build for their offspring. When or where does man give proof of any instinct to construct something beautiful and useful for the protection of the individual? When do adults even abandon their selfish interests in order to do something to further the survival of the species? It is not the individual that counts, but the survival of future generations.

In human society only religion, in which we find a summary of many mysteries, of factors unknown elsewhere, gives proof of any lofty concern for the human species, and that is why we often feel the need to call on religion for help.

It has been customary to make a clear distinction between two groups of animal instincts—those having to do with the protection of the species and those having to do with the protection of the individual.

In our social life, in our social activities, the one instinct that has operated is that leading the adult to protect the physical well-being of his infant. The child in and of himself has been forgotten, and we have neglected to provide what is necessary for him to develop normally; for such development never takes place solely through the influence of the character-traits of the adult. An adequate explanation of the survival of the species and the existence of the individual requires that we consider how these two instincts operate together.

Fundamental errors have been made in the organization of human life. Basic needs have been neglected, and human beings have lacked guidance from the moment they were born. A great mistake has been made. The child, a helpless little creature who does not possess the power of reason, has been thought to be of no importance, since we customarily think that the only thing that matters is a human will focused on an external goal. Thus the child, who is unable to pursue conscious, self-chosen goals in a hostile and unfamiliar world, has no importance in the eyes of adults.

It is curious to note the place that religion has generally assigned to the adoration of the Mother of Jesus, of the Holy Mother and Child; this would appear to be the expression of an intuitive truth that has found no concrete embodiment in everyday life.

Biologists today consider life to be intimately related to the existence of the earth as a whole. This concept can shed light on the need for a social order, for this view is closer to the truth than the common notion, which holds that living creatures are forced to conform to nature and bring about changes in their species through their efforts to do so. This is the conclusion at which those who view life as a struggle for survival and a process of adaptation have stopped. But there is another view, a broader view of life, that will lead us to a different conclusion.

To what environment must we adapt? To the earth, the soil, the continent on which we live. The earth must be regarded as having been created by animal life, for the earth's soil as presently constituted is the work of forms of animal life. How can the air and the sea remain pure and their chemical composition unchanged? Why don't the oceans become a solid mass because of the calcium carbonate constantly deposited in them by rivers? It is plant life that maintains the balance of the atmosphere, and it is animal life that maintains the balance of the oceans. Various corals extract calcium carbonate from water and use it to construct atolls and reefs.

Living creatures create a universal balance. Animals and plants are not forms of life that are separate from their environment and merely adapt to it mechanically. One might say that life is the force that creates the world.

Life sustains life. Animals are workers that create, purify, and maintain their environment. They do not do what they do for themselves; the ultimate end they pursue is not preserving their species in and of itself, but preserving the world. It is true that the direct aim of their actions is the survival of the species, and that they are motivated by the instinct to preserve the individual and the species, but they also serve a higher purpose. Animals not only act to preserve the species; they also do much more—they create the world.

Some functions appear to be absolutely necessary for the survival of the individual. Certain animals eat constantly, sometimes feeding on disgusting things. The earthworm, for example, eats dirt. If the earthworm's goal were to adapt to its environment, why couldn't it eat something else? But it consumes dirt continually, not for itself, but to transform the earth, to create soil.

Cows graze continually, eating quantities of fresh grass. They have been on the earth since very early times and have had to adapt to the food they eat by developing special organs —four stomachs. Couldn't cows eat something else? This species of animal might be likened to a chemical laboratory. The cow is a machine that runs constantly, and with only a little effort it can produce impressive quantities of milk. This is a necessary labor in the earth's economy.

As they seek nectar from flowers, insects spread pollen.

The instinct to preserve their kind causes bees to build amazing constructions.

Some animals eat putrefying carrion, thus fulfilling the function of cleaning up the environment. They add to the sacred scarab's beneficial activity serving the same purpose.

It is interesting that men have worshiped these animals. The people of India consider cows sacred, and the ancient Egyptians worshiped the scarab. Men have intuitively realized that these animals have a sacred function. How then could man, the intelligent being, the being possessed of a hand that is a free tool, an executive organ of his mind, not have a goal to fulfill in the world?

It is said that man's destiny is to enjoy creation, but he cannot! Enjoy what? The world? This is not his nature. What he seeks is not enjoyment, but labor and sacrifice. Man has a higher end, which is neither the enjoyment of material well-being nor even the survival of the species. If the ultimate end of animals is not that circumscribed, man will be even less satisfied to pursue such a limited goal. He has undoubtedly intuited this truth in the depths of his soul, even though he has banished it from his everyday life and made it the province of religion.

The fundamental goal of human existence is neither the survival of the individual nor that of the species. The individual adult's efforts to ensure his own survival and that of the species is only a means and a part of the task he must complete to fulfill his mission, to achieve his essential goal, to justify his reason for being—the creation of the environment.

Man may be destined to enjoy. He may be born to be the king of the universe. But he cannot reach this goal if he remains merely one of the creatures that inhabit the earth. He must live to realize his life's purpose, which is not visible in this world nor evident in nature. He advances toward his goal without seeing it, and this goal of which he is not aware is the construction of something superior to nature. Man works toward this goal without realizing it, however, and his lack of awareness causes him to feel bewildered and empty. He does his work in the cosmos painfully and laboriously, rather than with joy and relief. No one can exempt himself from the enormous task life sets him; he can merely choose whether he will fulfill it painfully or joyfully. If man understood his mission and knowingly and wisely obeyed the laws of his own existence, he would suddenly discover that he could change his life and experience joy where today he experiences only great difficulties.

As I have said, our observation of children has made us realize that work is man's fundamental instinct and that the child can work from morning till night without ever feeling tired, as if his labor were part of the order of nature.

Fatigue is not natural. It is not the result of work, but of working the wrong way. The child does his work without getting tired and proves to us that we have immense untapped energies.

It is obvious that man is born to work both with his hands and with his mind. This makes man the creator unique, and his hands and his mind must do their work together in functional unity. We have evidence that man has worked ever since human life began. Man has a different way of working compared with other forms of life. He does not always do the same thing; unlike corals, for example, he does not have a static cycle of life and work.

Man has taken upon himself every possible task in the world—the tasks of all the animals, of all inanimate things, of water, and of air. Man is able to adapt to any form of labor and make all forms his own. He is able to divide the work to be done among a number of individuals.

His love of his environment suggests what work he shall choose. Something calls to him to fulfill his mission. Man then works with a true spirit of sacrifice and by his work transforms the environment, creating another world that pervades all of nature. This world is something more than nature, for to build it man uses everything that exists in nature. Man creates a supernature. And man's supernature is different from ordinary nature.

Why are beehives called a work of nature while the paved roads built by man are not? Why does a cow belong to nature while a chemical retort does not? Why is the way our surroundings purify themselves "natural"? Because man goes further. He creates artificial things in nature. He extracts water from rocks and carries it to living creatures. He mines the earth for iron, coal, gold, and precious stones and brings them to the surface.

Man is the creator of a supernature. He is the master of matter. Today he even wrests from the universe what nature herself could never have given him. He has learned to exploit sources of energy lying deep below the surface of the earth and is using them for the creation of the supernature. He has tamed lightning and is working miracles. He is beginning to conquer the sky above. But he is aware only of individual phenomena and his mind does not grasp their essence. He does not see the great ultimate purpose of this conquest, the creation of supernature.

Through his efforts to accomplish all this, man has transformed himself. Particularly in recent times, something new has appeared in man. He is more intelligent now, but the feelings that should accompany this increase in intelligence are still missing, and they cannot stir within him because his way of life is wrong. He is overcome with hatred and does not obey the laws of nature. Nobler feelings—awareness of the unity of all living beings, for instance—are very slowly appearing in him. But harmony has yet to be achieved.

Man is the master of the entire earth. He transforms his environment and brings it under his control. He has assured his victory from the very first by creating human culture and human civilization. Human personality, too, has been changing, and we have witnessed the advent of the spirit of heroism, sacrifice, and dedication. As supernature is being constructed, the evolution of humanity is also taking place, representing not only further evolution of nature, but also a development of human personality. These conquests have been the work of a handful of men. Writing, for example—that supernatural gift—has been passed on by a few men to others, enabling mankind to record the products of the human intellect and to transmit them through the ages. The mathematical mind is also essential. Without it, progress would scarcely be conceivable. The child must therefore find a teacher able to develop his higher instincts. In this sense education is an interchange between human nature and supernature. It should indeed be taken into account that the man of our day is not simply the anatomical man of nature. He grows, thanks to a construction of the advancing and mechanical intelligence of man.

We could no longer live within nature if we could only walk with our feet and look with our eyes. Everything depends on the possibility of our going beyond our natural limitations. A preparation for this new order of life is therefore necessary, and that is why there is a need for education.

The man of supernature is no longer the man of nature. Having discovered how to tap enormous energies, he has to learn how to use them, to make them subservient to his life task, to set them to work. He has created a miraculous supernature by harnessing and using the energies of nature. And this very creation has made man a prodigious being, who sees and listens and rises above matter.

Man has also worked another miracle, which is the basis of everything and the key to everything, the greatest miracle of all, but also the one of which he is most unaware. Man has raised the level of human intelligence. Men can communicate with one another with amazing ease. In the course of human history men have organized into larger and larger groups, so that today all mankind is a single group. They are not conscious of this, yet it is a reality. All mankind today shares a common function. No longer are there separate groups of human beings, as was the case until just yesterday. A single interest unites them and causes them to function as a single living organism. No phenomeon can affect one human group without affecting others as a consequence. To put it a better way, the interest of any one group is the interest of all. We cannot speak of a center of civilization today, for civilization is spreading everywhere and there is no way of escaping it. There is no place for the thief to hide, and there are no more exiles. All mankind forms a single organism, but man continues to live in an emotional world that is outdated. Humanity today forms a single, indivisible unit—a *single nation*.

This single nation has opened the whole world and brought all men together. The earth's riches now belong to all. The fear of poverty must disappear, but once free of this fear man must realize that riches must no longer be sought within or on the surface of the earth. The single treasure of man, the raw material that promises to yield man everything, is human intelligence, an inexhaustible treasure.

That is why education must concern itself not only with the protection of personality, but also with guiding man toward the treasures that will ensure him a happy life—the intelligence of humanity and a normal human personality. We must not waste even one ounce of this wealth; we must hoard it as the riches of the earth were hoarded in the past.

Intelligence, a balanced personality, and the unity of all mankind as a single organism are man's wealth. What is therefore needed today is an education that will lead the human personality to recognize man's grandeur.

14 The Education of the Individual

A characteristic feature of our time is the gap between the high level reached by our outward civilization, which has been rapidly evolving in recent years, and the low level of human development, which has been raised very little since the earliest days of mankind.

In order to reestablish the proper balance, mankind must make a common effort to so enhance the dignity of the human personality that it will reach the same advanced level as the environment that man's labor and intelligence have created.

Education thus has assumed great importance today, and its role must no longer be limited to furthering the progress of material civilization, which may indeed have become too highly developed.

We must make an immediate collective effort to foster the development of personality. Such an effort will not be forthcoming simply because educators advocate it. All mankind must subconsciously be impelled to move forward. Education today operates in the same time-hallowed way everywhere; it follows a single narrow path and therefore cannot bring about the development of personality.

What needs to be done?

It is not so easy to answer this question as it is to pose it.

119

There is no such thing as a singleness of purpose, because there is no clear awareness of what work ought to be done.

Let us begin by attempting to clarify a few fundamental concepts. Exactly what is personality? The usual descriptions are vague, and a clear-cut distinction must be made between personality and individuality. The basic premises are not well defined, and the main problem is knowing what ought to be developed.

Here, as in so many other cases, we must have recourse to the child and ask him to shed light on what we are trying to understand. Such light can come to us only if we go back to the very beginning, to a point still very close to nothingness. Only the child can guide us, and he can do so only after we have prepared our inner selves to follow him. He will then lead us from nothingness to the beginning, and from the beginning to the development that follows. The child teaches us an important thing that education as a rule has failed to understand and to apply in practice. He has shown us the basis of the entire development of the personality of man, that superior individual whose potential seems almost unlimited and whose personality decidedly does not have a fixed limit set to its development. There is a very practical factor responsible for this open-endedness of the human personality—the development of individuality, which takes place independently of the influence of other human beings.

The child has shown us the basic principle underlying the process of education, which he has expressed in the words "Teach me to do things by myself!" The child resists letting adults help him if they try to substitute their own activity for his. The adult must help the child do things entirely on his own, for if the child does not reach the point of ceasing to rely on the help of adults and becoming independent, he will never fully mature intellectually or morally.

Psychoanalysis supports this fact and indicates the need for a new psychological approach. Psychoanalysts tell us that a person who is too attached to and dependent on someone else comes to feel that he can do nothing without the help of that person and may fall prey to a number of extremely distressing psychic illnesses. He cannot be cured of them unless he can overcome this psychological dependence.

Individual freedom is the basis of all the rest. Without such freedom it is impossible for personality to develop fully. Freedom is the key to the entire process, and the first step comes when the individual is capable of acting without help from others and becomes aware of himself as an autonomous being. This is a rudimentary definition of freedom and one that appears to be at odds with the social nature of man and the functioning of the human collectivity. How can the idea of individual freedom and that of life in society be reconciled, since the latter is fraught with restrictions that force the individual to obey the laws of the collectivity? The same problem, the same apparent contradiction, seems to characterize our everyday life in society. Yet freedom is the necessary foundation of organized society. Individual personality could not develop without individual freedom.

We find ourselves lost at this point in a maze of contradictions. Only the child can light our path through it. The child is our only guide to what education should be; only he can help us understand the complications of social life and man's unconscious aspiration to be free in order that he may bring about a better social order. Man seeks freedom in order to build a supernatural society. He does not seek freedom in order to go his own way, but in order to live.

We must call on biology, which has revealed many secrets of life that long remained hidden, if we want a clearer picture of the relationship between the individual and society. Let us reflect on the evolution of animal life. Primitive species of animal life form colonies, in which a number of individuals function as a single organism. An example is the coelenterates. Some members of the colony perform the function of digestion, while others defend it against outside enemies. A number of individuals thus functions as a single unit of life in this phylum. The scale of evolution starts where individuals begin to live their own lives.

Only individuals can unite to form a society. Ants, for example, form a society composed of an enormous number of individuals—an impossibility in the case of more primitive forms of animal life.

Separate individuals are complex and are capable of banding together in huge numbers. They may form not only an aggregate, but a real association based on distribution of the labor necessary to fulfill the society's functions. Association takes place when the group engages in collective activities, as when birds undertake their vast migrations. They form an association of free individuals.

The fundamental freedom—the freedom of the individual—is necessary for the evolution of a species for two reasons: (1) it gives individuals infinite possibilities for growth and improvement and constitutes the starting point of man's complete development; (2) it makes the formation of a society possible, for freedom is the basis of human society.

We must make it possible for the individual to be free and independent. The key to this complex problem is to furnish means for development of the free personality that have to do with the environment as well. The environment must promote not only the freedom of the individual, but also the formation of a society. The education of humanity must rest on a scientific foundation and follow from it every step of the way.

The first step has been taken in our schools, which have

given the child the possibility of teaching us this great, revealing lesson and helping us pursue this goal scientifically. The first step, from which all the rest follow, is then to help the child develop all his functions as a free individual and to foster that development of personality that actuates social organization.

The drive for freedom, the individual's inherent need to be let alone so that he can act on his own, determines what we call one "level of education." It is in fact the first level of education, properly speaking. In our view this level is the province of the school, the elementary school, for materials that foster the freely organized activity of the child must be furnished. The second level leads to society, to the social organization of the adult. Secondary school should be the gateway to a development of personality and social organization.

These are, then, two levels, or planes, of development of human life if the aim of education is to contribute to the formation of man and his personality, raise humanity to the point where it can make genuine progress, and save mankind.

The aim of this approach is to raise mankind to the same level of development as the environment and thus eliminate the imbalance between them. Education is indispensable not to foster material progress but to save humanity, and all our efforts must be directed toward helping the inner man form himself rather than fighting against the outside world. We must ponder long and hard and work to deepen our knowledge of human psychology and education so that they may become a true help to man. The aim of education should not be to teach how to use human energies to improve the environment, for we are finally beginning to realize that the cornerstone of education is the development of the human personality, and that in this regard education is of immediate importance for the salvation of mankind.

If this is what education is, our first concern need no

longer be school administration, courses of study, and so on. The school curriculum will always be an aid in education, but it must not be forced on mankind in the name of some unconscious goal. Mankind must bring the aim of education into the full light of consciousness. Education today does not take personality into account and does not develop it. It is motivated by a point of view that is not only wrong but dangerous, based on a false premise that represents a real peril for mankind. Man today pays no heed to human personality and regards human society as a colony without individuals. He knows only dependence and submissiveness, which kill personality. Our ideas are so confused that we think that there is a contradiction between the free personality and society. We keep asking, "Once there are free personalities, what will become of society?"

We must do away with this misconception, for it puts us in imminent danger. It has come about because we have had no clear notion of what organized society really is. This misconception weaves a web of errors in the way of man's progress and perhaps even threatens his survival.

We are coming to realize that we must give men their freedom, that we must educate the masses, that we must educate all men. A wordless cry has been raised for us to see things clearly as they really are—a cry to defend man.

The levels of education must have a foundation, a human aim—the progressive development of the child's personality, which our experience with him has made us see in an entirely new light; for the child who is free to act and to do so without being influenced by the suggestion exercised by the adult shows us the real laws of human life.

I will discuss the four levels of education that we discern. It was not I who made this fourfold distinction, nor was it the child. It is based on the orderly pattern of development. We adults live amid absolute disorder, and we have succeeded in making frightful chaos the basis of our organization of society.

The human being proves to have a fundamental need for order from the very first years of his life. He is eager to live in orderly surroundings, and he disciplines himself when he can act freely and follow the dictates of his nature. It is not the adult who teaches him this, for the adult has no notion of this sort of discipline, because his development has been constrained. We should remember what the Bible says, "Great things are found among men: kings and riches, but something never seen is inner discipline." This is the cause of the fall of many civilizations.

Discipline is the fundamental instinct of man, as children prove to us. It is a normal need of human nature when it is protected and not deflected from its natural path.

When we speak of the free man we must above all correct some mistaken ideas. It is inaccurate to say that the free man is at odds with society, with order, and with social discipline. If we help man follow the design of normal development and follow his own natural laws, we will bring about a more perfect society than the one we now have. We are against the artificial programs that make man a slave. This does not mean, however, that we are against order and discipline, which are true laws of mankind. I speak in the name of my Lord, the child.

The child, a free human being, must teach us and teach society order, calm, discipline, and harmony. When we help him, love blossoms, too—the love of which we have great need to bring men together and create a happy life.

The aim of education is not to teach facts; education has remained at an absurdly inferior level by comparison with the progress man has made in other fields. I believe that it will seem inconceivable in the near future that education was so narrowly circumscribed that it made the solution of social problems impossible. There is good reason to regard education as a tyrannical and dictatorial coercion exercised over every aspect of children's lives; this tyrannical power is pointless and benefits no one. It makes even less sense and has even less point in these times when man has such an intense desire for freedom. It is difficult for us even to conceive of the slavery that prevents man from being himself, that cuts off at the very roots the human personality we so desperately need. The simple truth, as our experience has amply demonstrated, is that the laws the child is forced to obey are arbitrary and that he must no longer be subject to them, so that the laws of life may guide his development. Programs can be changed; the laws of life are immutable. If we base education on the laws of life, we will create genuine levels of education rather than mere curricula.

Individual freedom is the basis of the first level of education. Our aim must be to make the child capable of acting by himself, as we have already indicated. The adult must be a source of help, not an obstacle. Above all, he must aid the child, never make him the helpless victim of a blind authority that does not take his real goal into account. We must truly help fulfill the child's needs; we must let him do things by himself because his very life depends on his being able to act. He must be allowed to function freely. A human being who cannot carry out his vital functions becomes sick, and we often find that children who are not allowed to develop normally suffer psychic illnesses.

We must not only offer children personal help; we must also provide them with the right environment, for their proper development depends on vital activity in and on the environment. Science has taught us that the aim of the new pedagogy must be to create the proper environment for development. Our position is very far removed from that of many people who think that the adult should not do anything with regard to the child. Should we perhaps leave the child all alone and abandon him?

We who live within supernature cannot live within nature. We have done nothing for the supernature of the child, whereas lower forms of animal life do a great deal for their offspring. The human being who has not been psychologically crippled has very demanding requirements that need to be met if he is to develop his free personality, but we keep the child shut up in our homes and do all sorts of things in his stead when we should furnish him the means of doing them by himself. The supernatural environment needed by the child and the adolescent must be created for them until they enter our adult social life themselves. It is up to us to construct such an environment to protect our offspring.

This is the mission of education. Let us therefore unite our efforts to construct an environment that will allow the child and the adolescent to live an independent, individual life in order to fulfill the goal that all of us are pursuing—the development of personality, the formation of a supernatural order, and the creation of a better society. The human soul must shape itself within a supernatural milieu.

The child must therefore have his own special environment and the adult must help him. This opens the gates to the practical realm of education. What must be done? What must the adult do? Stop telling the child little stories? Stop letting children have fun and stop allowing them to participate in sports? People sometimes think that the sort of freedom the child should be given is the freedom to live a terribly serious sort of life, and the one goal of modern education has been to prevent this.

But isn't it possible that life really is a very serious matter? The life of freedom is not at all frivolous, as we learn once again from the child, who seeks to do practical, difficult, and serious things—positive things—and is happy when he can do useful things, for the human being seeks to climb higher and higher and to pursue a definite goal.

Vast instruction and an environment that meets his needs are necessary to develop the human soul and human intelligence—the life of the child.

We have been wrongly accused of wanting to deprive children of joy! But our intention is neither to give them joy nor to take it away. Quite the contrary. The child in our prepared environment does not play. He works, and greed disappears; he works, and laziness disappears. He wants to do everything! He is a precocious human being by comparison with other children. The human individual has demonstrated a tendency to work independently in order to develop his mind, and then love is born and leads to a happy society.

Man does not find happiness in play as an activity apart from life. Those who know how to do nothing else but amuse themselves soon fall victim to depression. Our schools, whose duty it is to make possible the happy life that is man's natural condition, must provide the child with surroundings appropriate to his needs—buildings and furniture on his scale—and at the same time put before him noble ideas and great discoveries of the human mind, offering him in material form the abstractions that are the typical products of the adult intellect so that the loftiest creations of human intelligence may penetrate his mind.

The child must rise to the higher order of the spirit through concrete things. When we put before him the greatest ideas and discoveries of the human mind, he will be stimulated and his enthusiasm will be aroused. He will show a wonderful persistence in his work and never feel fatigue. It is obvious that the individual works hard to develop his own personality. Every human being has his own interests in mind (though perhaps not in any conscious way); every individual acts in his own interest. The child is thought to be a selfish creature. But he is not selfish in this regard. Selfishness enters the picture only with regard to seeking possessions and power. The selfishness of the child is that of the man who seeks to withdraw from society and dwell apart from others in order to live the life of a hermit and cultivate his own soul.

How can we cultivate human individuality without living apart?

The first period of life is that in which the individual must develop *by himself,* independently. This is the period of self-education. Children naturally feel helpless in a hostile world that overwhelms them. They need protection, not tyranny. When the adult gives the child something, he does so to secure some advantage for himself. This constitutes a form of tyranny. Even when he is free, the child still feels the need for protection. He needs and seeks encouragement; he has no false pride and goes to adults to show them his work. He is pleased if he has done well and pleased to see what he has accomplished. He needs encouragement to go on with his difficult task—the development of his personality, the vital work of an embryo.

The characteristic feature of the education given the child, at this stage in his life must therefore be the safeguarding of his freedom, and since he is living in an artificial environment, he must be surrounded by things tailored to his needs. Everything must be child-size, but not in the sense of mechanically reducing the physical scale of adult things. A whole world just his size must be created for the child. This concept may be illustrated by the way religion should be taught to children if religious education is desired for them at this time. Religion should be presented in terms of God's protection of the individual. The child has a guardian angel always watching over him, an angel who is definitely not a tyrant. The child prays God to watch over him and his loved ones. He prays for personal protection. The child knows that there is Someone who watches over him, who loves him, who protects him. To a child this is a natural view of God, for it is a reflection of his life as a child. This conception is shared by adults who have not fully matured intellectually and who seek in religion only protection. In adults it represents a form of arrested development.

If secondary education, however, is set up along the very same lines as this first level, it goes against nature, for once the child has passed the age appropriate to his formation as an individual he needs to devote himself to the formation of his personality.

The level of education must be changed at this point. The adolescent's social formation must now begin, and the individual must be given social experience.

It is not true that universities are a preparation for social life. All schools today are obstacles to the proper formation of the individual for social life.

How is social education possible if adolescents must remain shut up in a mass prison? The young person then has no such thing as a social life. There are enormous contradictions. Schools do not prepare young people for social life but rather for earning a living. They train young people for a trade or a profession. And all of them exercise their trade or practice their profession like slaves. This really means that we replace true social life with a degrading caricature of it. We cannot keep a society that is threatening to fall to pieces intact with men whose only training is in a trade that will earn them a living. We need *whole men*. Such men will be quite capable of earning their living in a better society, of course, and it is necessary to pass on a rather large body of knowledge to young people directly, for the human mind is very receptive during the formative years. But only the barest minimum of knowledge is given to him, and that is too little. This is a serious error. We must follow a different path.

Young people at present cannot acquire social experience because they are forced to devote all their time to studying. In order for the adolescent to acquire social experience, society must build the right sort of environment for him, a supernature suited to his needs where he can have effective, practical experience of every aspect of social life.

Independence on another level is required at this age, for independence is necessary in social life as well. Young people must perform social functions independently, work, and earn a living. Society must furnish a special environment in which young people can earn their livelihood. They must have this opportunity because they will one day have to help build supernature. They must therefore be given the chance to spend time studying and practicing manual and intellectual skills. But they must not be forced to study every minute, for this is a form of torture that causes mental illness. The human personality must be given a chance to realize every one of its capabilities. Men today are forced to take up either a trade or a profession. We might say that those who work only with their minds are *mutilated* men and those who work only with their hands *decapitated* men. We try to create a harmony between those who work with their minds and those who work with their hands by appealing to their sentiments, but there is a need for whole men. Every side of the human personality must function. A young person may have special aptitudes in some direction, but the choice of which aptitudes to foster must be made individually. There will always be individual differences, but they are not paramount. The aim of human development must be a total expression of life, a life superior to ours. Then we will reach a higher level.

That is the third level, in fact, characterized by the preparation of the human soul for work as the vital function that is the cornerstone of social experience. When he enters the workaday world, man must be aware first and foremost of his social responsibility. If he is not, we will have not only men without heads and without hands, but also men who are selfish, who have no consciences, who are irresponsible members of society. In a society such as ours, full of complications and dangers, this is an enormous responsibility. It is therefore necessary to prepare men to be aware of it and to fulfill it.

Universities confer degrees after students have passed examinations, but often the student passes by sheer luck. Society admits into its ranks men of whom it has little knowledge and who have no conscience. The real examinations should be spiritual ones. The student should be asked to demonstrate his ability by showing the kind of work he can do. The candidates could thus prove their worth and be recognized as men of value to society. They would then have a sense of responsibility and take it as a guide for their lives. But here we abandon the schoolroom and open the gate of life.

The fourth level is life itself. We eventually leave school and the teaching that keeps young people in lock step, drives them on without their knowing where they are going, abandons them after a specified number of years, and dumps them onto society without bothering about them again. Where will they learn the things they don't know? What guarantee can they offer the society that daily turns out men with deaf consciences—mutilated men?

All mankind must be united and remain united forever. The masses must be educated, and education must be available at all times. On this fourth level society must help every human being and keep all mankind at the same high level as the evolving environment, and then elevate man above the environment so that he may further perfect it as he perfects himself.

IV

Address to the
World Fellowship of Faiths

15   Educate for Peace

A fundamental principle of peace is at work in the very fact that this association is meeting together here, for peace is not, we might say, the rational work of man, but rather a work of creation. The forces that create the world are precisely the forces that must create peace.

All humanity that works for the common good, even though it may be unaware of it, is creating the new world that must be the world of peace. The great efforts of men who have labored, made discoveries, studied, and suffered—all the work of mankind will be seen to have had one common purpose in the world that will be the world of peace.

Even if men are fighting one another today or have fought in the past, even if they have waged wars and lined up on opposing sides of the battlefield, they have nonetheless all been working throughout history to build a world that will be the world of peace.

Men are better than they appear to be. Indeed, human beings impress me as being extremely good and charitable, but they practice goodness and charity so unconsciously that mankind does not realize that it possesses these virtues. It

This address was given to the World Fellowship of Faiths in London on July 28, 1939.

137

might be said that human strife and men's inability to understand one another are surface phenomena, and that beneath
that surface there have been immeasurable depths of
goodness and sacrifice in men's hearts throughout the ages, a
goodness and a spirit of sacrifice that history has hidden and
of which humanity is unaware.[1]

The truth at times appears to be made up of apparent contradictions. If this apparent contradiction did not exist, the
truth would be easier to grasp. Everyone must search for the

---

[1]These words of Maria Montessori take on a wider and clearer
meaning if we consider her later remarks on the role of man's
self-sacrifice in her vast philosophical conception of the cosmos
that her listeners glimpsed more than once. The following ex-
cerpts from a lecture she gave in Rome in 1946 are moving
evidence of her views:

So: the immeasurable depths of man's goodness!

A good man to us is—as Christ taught—a man who lays down
his life for his friends. Goodness means self-sacrifice, a lifelong
sacrifice. This goodness is within the hearts of all men, and it is
not by their good intentions but by their labor that we recognize it.

Men do not work to fulfill their own needs but to fulfill the
needs of others. Let us consider the baker, for example. While
others sleep, he stays up to bake bread that will be ready when
the others awaken. Does he bake the bread for himself? Neither
he nor his family will eat all of it. The baker works and
sacrifices for others. Does he do so just one night or two? No;
this self-sacrifice lasts all his life.

Let us consider the miner who extracts coal from the earth.
He gives up sunlight and fresh air and buries himself alive; he
knows that he may lose his life in an explosion at any moment.
When he bids his children goodbye in the morning, he is not

truth because it is hidden, yet it exists. *This is what sustains man's soul: the certainty that the truth he seeks does exist.*

On this earth, where the adult rules and oversees the distribution of the world's goods, it would appear that men are all at odds with one another. Even in an area in which personal interests are further in the background and in which men ought to feel closer to truth and reality—that is, in their practice of religion—even there they disagree. It is the aim and the mission of this association to seek interfaith har-

---

certain whether he will get back home alive. A hero. And not a hero during just one battle, but a hero who sacrifices his entire life. He certainly cannot use all the coal he brings to the surface just to heat his own home or cook his own food. The coal is for the use of countless people who are unknown to him, who can't even thank him for his sacrifice. The coal will be used in furnaces that the miner will never see, and thus he will never have the satisfaction of witnessing the results of his sacrifice.

This hero obeys perfectly Christ's command, Let not thy right hand know what thy left hand doeth.

And those who work the land by the sweat of their brows do so in order that the grain and the fruit that they grow, the wood that they hew in the forest may be consumed by men who live far away. And those who mill grain, those who transport fruit and flowers long distances reap no thanks.

This universal charity is not like a deliberate act of charity, which requires some concrete motivation such as seeing the suffering and the needs of the poor. It is not an occasional or sporadic sort of charity that ceases once the expected thanks from the beneficiaries is forthcoming.

No, cosmic charity is universal. It requires the lifelong dedication of each man to all mankind, the rich man and the poor man alike. It does not relieve some particular form of misery. It lifts up the hearts of all men and helps civilization rise to a mony, to show that all religions desire the same thing and love in the same way. That is why your prayers have borrowed words from all the world's religions and why they have been found to fit together perfectly. Another aim of this association is to make all men on earth, whatever their religious beliefs, tenets, and practices, realize that they are intimately one and could call one another brother or friend.

We are very much aware of this truth and this unity, and who is not? In ancient days the philosophers, men who knew how to rise above their narrow personal concerns, were aware that men can call one another friend, can understand one another, and can be at peace with one another. We must ask ourselves, Why is it that the more men study and improve their minds, the more beautiful things they discover or

---

higher level as it ensures the existence of each and all. The depths of this goodness and dedication are thus boundless.

It will be objected that these people do not work for the good of others; they labor only to earn their livelihoods in order to live as enjoyable lives as possible. That is true; that is the conscious part of it. But unconsciously they are carrying out the work of creation. They are obeying an unconscious command that rules events and preserves life everywhere in the universe.

The trees that purify the air, the herbs that capture vitamins from sunlight, the coral that filters the sea, which teems with countless creatures that would die if there were no such forms of life to keep the water pure, the animals that populate the earth are unconscious of their cosmic mission, but without them the harmony of creation would not exist and life would cease. They do all this because of the vital instincts impelling them to eat and breathe in order to continue to live.

This harmony, based on the needs of each and all, is of divine origin. That is why man has no conception of it and perceives only his own immediate needs. But if man could raise his concreate, the more strife there is among them? This, too, is a mystery. Why are all men in their hearts conscious of this unity, and why is there this dissension among them on the surface? Because men must live in the everyday world and bow to its demands, some might answer. It cannot be denied that men are different from one part of the world to another, that they have hidebound traditions that are different from one place to another, that there is no prayer powerful enough, no logical argument persuasive enough to make them will to understand one another. But might there not be a new path that could be followed? Might there not be a new being in whom we may place all our hopes? Yes. The child. From the religious point of view, the child is the most powerful being in the world. We cannot doubt that there is com-

---

sciousness to a higher level he would awaken and be aware of the disinterested goodness and self-sacrifice of his fellows.

If we educate children to see this, they will ready themselves to feel gratitude toward all mankind. This is an affective aspect of our "cosmic education."

When we send children to buy things in a store, pens and paper for instance, we say, "Look, that person waiting on you is here to help you. She works here all day long, waiting on you and all the other customers who come into the store. When you buy something, she thanks you with a smile. You must feel grateful to her and appreciate what a good person she is."

At mealtime the children pray, "Dear Lord, bless the unknown men who have obeyed thy will and worked for us and given us this food." In this way the child comes to have an all-embracing sense of humanity and justice.

The aim of such an education indicates the desire to contribute to the good of all, to share in this cosmic goodness, and to offer God the obedient service that unites us with him in his work of creation.

munication between him and the Creator. He is the Creator's most evident handiwork. We may say that the child is the most religious being in the human world.

If we wish to discover a pure being, a being who has neither philosophical ideas nor a political ideology and is equally removed from both, we will find this neutral being in the child. And if we think that men are different because they speak different languages, we will recognize in the child a being who speaks no language and who is ready to learn to speak any language at all. This child must therefore be our central focus when we seek ways to peace. Why do we not call upon children? Why do not triumphant bands of children appear at meetings where the problem of peace is being discussed? If processions of children appeared among us—companies of those human beings who represent the living possibility of peace—we would have to welcome them reverently and bow down before them in admiration. The child would appear among us as the teacher of peace. We must gather around him to learn the mystery of humanity, to discover in him the mystery of a fundamental goodness that our outer lives and acts belie. That is the source of the knowledge that interests us most of all. If we truly yearn for brotherhood and understanding among men, there must also be brotherhood and understanding between the adult and the child!

If children are the teachers of love, we need not go out and look for them. Let us remember that every family has children and that in every family this. principle of love is therefore at work. When a child is born into a family, his mother becomes a more beautiful woman and his father a better man; and if the child already creates this atmosphere of love simply by coming into this world, he then goes on to disclose those laws of growth that reveal the roots of human personality and human greatness to those who observe him carefully. The child possesses immeasurable abilities and un-suspected powers of intelligence. His heart is so sensitive to the need for justice that we must call him, as Emerson also did, "the Messiah who forever returns to dwell among fallen men, to lead them to the Kingdom of Heaven."

We are convinced that the child can do a great deal for us, more than we can do for him. We adults are rigid. We remain in one place. But the child is all motion. He moves hither and thither to raise us far above the earth. Once I felt this impression very strongly, more deeply than ever before, and I took almost a vow to become a follower of the child as my teacher. Then I saw before me the figure of the child, as those close to me now see and understand him. We do not see him as almost everyone else does, as a helpless little creature lying with folded arms and outstretched body, in his weakness. We see the figure of the child who stands before us with his arms held open, beckoning humanity to follow.